# HOW ODDS EVEN THROUGH GRACE

## HENRY HEARNS

KP PUBLISHING COMPANY

Copyright 2024 by Henry Hearns

*When Odds Even Through Grace*

All rights reserved. In accordance with the U.S. Copyright Act of 1976, the scanning, uploading, and electronic sharing of any part of this book without the permission of the publisher is unlawful piracy and theft of the author's intellectual property. If you would like to use material from this book (other than for review purposes), prior written permission must be obtained by contacting the publisher at info@kp-pub.com.

Thank you for your support of the author's rights.

ISBN: 978-1-960001-04-7 (Hardcover)
ISBN: 978-1-960001-05-4 (Paperback)
ISBN: 978-1-960001-06-1 (eBook)

Unless otherwise indicated, all Scriptures quotations are taken from the Holy Bible, King James Version (Public Domain)

Scripture taken from the New King James Version®. Copyright © 1982 by Thomas Nelson. Used by permission. All rights reserved.

Scriptures marked NIV are taken from the NEW INTERNATIONAL VERSION (NIV): Scripture taken from THE HOLY BIBLE, NEW INTERNATIONAL VERSION®. Copyright © 1973, 1978, 1984, 2011 by Biblica, Inc.™. Used by permission of Zondervan

Scripture quotations are from the ESV® Bible (The Holy Bible, English Standard Version®), Copyright © 2001 by Crossway, a publishing ministry of Good News Publishers. Used by permission. All rights reserved.

Published by:

KP Publishing Company
Publisher of Fiction, Nonfiction & Children's Books
Las Vegas, NV 89117
www.kp-pub.com

Printed in the United States of America

# DEDICATION

I dedicate this book to: Henry, Valeria, Hugo (deceased), Sylvia, and Sylvester (twins), and to my youngest, Angela.

This project started three years ago, and from that point on, my children have been there for me. They all have their own responsibilities, yet they kept me and this project in their prayers.

To my grandchildren:
- Avril
- Andrea
- Shanita
- Abigail
- Leah (Bonus granddaughter)

To my great-grands:
- Price-Wyatt
- Asher and Audra (twins)

***I love you!***

# CONTENTS

*Dedication* — v
*Endorsements* — xi
*Foreword #1* — xv
*Foreword #2* — xix
*Introduction* — xxi
*Preface* — xxiii

1. Breaking the Chains — 1
2. No Circumstance So Great — 5
   Mama — 5
   Daddy — 10
3. Finding Joy in Poverty — 13
4. A New Plantation—A New Season in My Life — 23
5. Overcoming Racial Tension — 31
   My Two Great Grandfathers—Former Slaves — 37
6. The Good and Gracious Samaritan — 43
7. Deacon Fetterson and How I Came to "Fess-a-ligion" — 51
8. Our Own Little Promised Land — 55
9. The Heart Knows—Essie (An Introduction) — 61

| | | |
|---|---|---|
| 10. | Onward Christian Soldier—The Army Calls | 67 |
| 11. | Divine Intervention—Korea | 77 |
| 12. | Running To Win The Prize—Tennessee State University | 89 |
| 13. | The Son Shines, Even Through the Clouds of Segregation | 99 |
| | California 1960–1964 | 99 |
| 14. | "Oh, Let Us Exalt His Name Together!" | 113 |
| 15. | Resurrected In Christ | 121 |
| 16. | The Heavens Declare His Glory | 127 |
| | Edwards AFB and Twenty Years of Service | 127 |
| 17. | The Death of Hope—1968 | 135 |
| 18. | Faith, Party, and Politics—Eighteen Years of Public Service | 149 |
| 19. | My Dearest Essie | 159 |
| 20. | Fatherhood | 165 |
| | Henry Jr. | 165 |
| | A Message From My Oldest Son, Henry Hearns, Jr. | 167 |
| | 2 My Sometimey Dad | 167 |
| | Valeria | 169 |
| | A Special Word From Valeria, My Oldest Daughter | 170 |
| | Theodore | 171 |
| | Sylvia and Sylvester—The Twins | 171 |
| | A Word From My Daughter, Sylvia | 172 |
| | A Word From My Youngest Son, Sylvester | 173 |
| | Angela | 174 |
| | A Special Thought From My Youngest, Angela | 175 |
| | From Andrea and Avril, Two of My Beloved Grandchildren | 176 |
| 21. | No Heart So Strong | 177 |

| | | |
|---|---|---|
| 22. | An Uncommon Kinship | 185 |
| 23. | The Things I've Seen and The Lessons I've Learned | 189 |
| | The Things I've Seen | 189 |
| | The Lessons I've Learned | 196 |
| 24. | Ninety-One and Counting | 203 |
| | *Acknowledgments* | *209* |

# ENDORSEMENTS

Raleigh B. Washington, DD, M.Div., President /CEO, PROMISE KEEPERS, National Office, P.O. Box 11798, Denver, CO 80211-0798

> *I have given virtually all of my life as a believer to the ministry of reconciliation. First, it was black and white on the west side of Chicago and has now evolved to the Biblical calling for reconciliation between Jewish and Gentile believers. As we continue to see racial conflict outside of and within the Church of Jesus Christ, there is need for a fresh approach. Bishop Hearns provides this compelling and fresh approach to reconciliation through the story of his own life. A must-read! You will fall in love with the Bishop and open your heart to reach out in a loving relationship with someone who is racially different than yourself.*

William T. Marshall, Ph.D., MFT, Founder and CEO, California Institute of Health & Social Services, Inc.

> *This Holy man of God came into my life in December 21, 2008, when a psychotherapist who worked in one of our California Institutes facilities in Lancaster, California, introduced him to me. During my first meeting with Bishop Hearns, he impressed me as a man with warmth and with a steadfast ideological and spiritual*

*input who has the theoretical underpinnings required for successful street productivity. We shared similar moments of family historical sharecropper history together, as well as our education and graduate studies. I began to follow this remarkable characteristic follower of Jesus. He has led community and church members as he guided them in the love of Jesus. I noted the acts of kindness that he has bestowed upon children and the leadership that he has provided young ministers and ministries in the Antelope Valley as well. Bishop has been and continues to exemplify the role of Jesus and the characteristics of love. I will continue to support this Man of God, who is relentless in teaching the word of God.*

In memory of William T. Marshall, Ph.D., whose faith and commitment to grace continue to inspire.

Hon. Howard P "Buck" McKeon, United States Representative, 25th Congressional District California, Chairman, House Armed Services Committee.

*It was late in the evening on October 1, 1958, when our train pulled into the station in San Antonio, Texas, where I would begin my two-and-a-half years of service as a missionary for the Church of Jesus Christ of Latter-day Saints. I was shocked to see the restrooms and drinking fountains were identified as "colored" and "white." I had never seen anything thing like that growing up in southern California, and I had never even met a black person. Over the years in business, community service, and finally, 22 years of serving in the House of Representatives, I now have many black friends and acquaintances. Henry was the first who taught me what it was really like growing up black in the South before civil rights laws were enforced. He was a black man who was forbidden to drink from the fountains or, use the restrooms or, sit in the front of the bus or eat in a restaurant because of his color. Things that I had never even thought about, he had lived with every day. He is a great man who has overcome much without holding feelings of bitterness or rancor. His total acceptance of Jesus Christ and His Atonement teaches all of us it's not the color of our skin but rather what comes from our heart and soul that determines what mark we will make in this life. Bishop Hearns, through the story of his life, gives us all hope in this life and the life to come. I am proud to call him friend and I commend his story to all.*

# FOREWORD #1

It is always a pleasure to hold in hand a book you believe will become a blessing to each person who reads it. *How Odds Even*, written by my dear friend Henry Hearns, will gift to its reader godly wisdom, as well as insights into hardships few of us ever will experience. I feel honored—honored to be given an invitation to write the "forewords," but even more honored to have been given the gift of Henry's friendship.

That said, I'm delighted to lead you into the pool that is *How Odds Even (Through Grace)*. The analogy of a "pool" seems appropriate for you are about to enter an experience of *genuine refreshing*. This book will lift and renew you the way a fresh breeze and cool water do during a mid-day summer heat wave. Relax in your favorite reading chair and allow this pleasant reprieve to affect the climate of your soul.

Twenty-five years ago, Henry, who was the first African-American mayor of Lancaster, California, invited me to speak at an event. Though I had never met him (Lancaster being on the far edge of Los Angeles County and my home being near the center, 50 miles away), I nonetheless accepted. I did so for two basic reasons. The first, because I'd heard Mr. Hearns was *both* mayor of Lancaster and senior pastor of one of largest congregations in the area. The second was that, as mayor, he'd proposed that his community provide a controversial event. Without fanfare or political pomp, and without any bravado, divisive threat, or political posturing, Mayor Hearns was proposing the city observe Dr. Martin Luther King Jr.'s birthday. He was doing so at a time when King's memory and birthday were still finding a foothold in hearts and on calendars of our nation as a nationally-recognized holiday and day of remembrance.

Thus, I accepted the invitation, feeling it a high honor to do so and especially honored to be able to stand side-by-side with an African-American pastor/mayor. I was hoping for the best but willing to face the worst, even if it was nothing more than a sign-wielding protester or a catcall from a bigot in the crowd. Thankfully, only the best occurred. I discovered a celebrative, positive crowd with a beautiful racial mix on hand and in numbers fully representative of the city's population-mix. Also, I discovered the large degree to which the mode, manor, method and mindset of Mayor Henry Hearns was an immeasurably decisive factor in this positive outcome. The mayor was a great deal of the reason for the health and harmony in this city, for not only was there a receptive spirit among the citizenry, but the mayor's role in leadership was doubtless the pivotal factor. *The city respected and trusted this man!*

They still do.

Even though Henry no longer serves as mayor, he is doubtless as trusted and welcomed a leader as lives in California's Antelope Valley. This peripheral but thriving area (160,000, 1/60th of Los Angeles County's population of nearly 10,000,000) heralds the quality and presence of former Mayor Bishop Henry Hearns. Though years continue to pass, his influence is admired and well-received. Indeed, returning to my analogy of the pool—it's *refreshing*.

This part of Henry's story is, however, by no means complete. I believe you move from one refreshing feature to another in this book. As the writing propels you through story after story, you will see clearly *how odds have evened* for this African-American man, and the message of applied *grace is* clear. Practical principles for living shine through with a radiance of meaning, and I believe you will be as amazed by the life of my dear friend as I have been.

But his story isn't over yet. Its impact continues to be seen, durably and ongoing, effecting goodness, generosity, and God's graciousness in and on his community today. Spiritually, educationally, culturally, sociologically, economically, you name it: Henry Hearns has been—and still is mind you—a positive and blessed influence wherever he goes, the heart and tender touch of his remarkable leadership a Godsend.

I must close, but please understand: what I have referenced is but the tip of an iceberg named Bishop Henry Hearns. The glory of it all is this:

*Henry never seeks the glory of personal recognition.*

Nonetheless, his is a *glorious* story, one that begins in Mississippi, decades past, when that southern state was the boiling pot of the racial prejudice, an injustice that found shameful influence to varying degrees throughout America. Thankfully, a lot has changed over the last 82 years in our beloved nation. But the bottom line fact is that neither legislative nor judicial influence is ever the whole story.

People like Henry Hearns have affected attitudinal changes in America, dynamic and lasting changes, as much as any law could bring about. Laws may mandate change, but only people who allow God to make them instruments of change to turn history on its head and even the odds can influence the mindset of a culture unto its transformation.

One last word of tribute to my friend:

I have never used this term with regard to any of my personal friends or mentors throughout the years, nor of any of the ongoing counselors, advisors, or teachers I've had over the span of my life. I'll use it for the first time here:

*Henry Hearns is my hero!*

Indeed! Having written it and said it aloud, I like that title. *Henry Hearns is heroic*, and I have no doubt you'll delight in reading about him and be *refreshed*.

Dr. Jack W. Hayford
Founder/Chancellor
The King's University
Dallas/Los Angeles

We would like to honor the memory of Jack W. Hayford, who passed on January 8, 2023, and whose words in this foreword continue to inspire.

# FOREWORD #2

Like so many others, my life has been enhanced by my association and friendship with Bishop Henry Hearns. He is a compassionate man of faith who exhibits a seriousness of purpose, perseverance, and sincere passion for justice. His presence fills the room; his faith in Christ permeates everything that he does. During the past two decades, he relayed some of his experiences in overcoming the life of a Mississippi sharecropper. He endured many years of extreme racial prejudice before becoming a very successful politician. However, it was not until I read his life story, as told in this autobiography, *How Odds Even Through Grace*, that I realized how he became an inspirational force.

As explained in his earliest chapters, aptly titled "Breaking the Chains," "No Circumstance So Great," and "Finding Joy in Poverty," Bishop Hearns tells the story of growing up under the dark cloud of poverty and prejudice. He was born on April 23, 1933, to Earnest and Birdie Hearns, who were sharecroppers in Byhalia, Mississippi. Through hard work and tolerance, his family eventually bought their own farm and began to make a life for themselves. However, their life on the farm was short-lived as the first of many difficult circumstances plagued the Hearns family.

Bishop Hearns gives this no-holds-barred account of his struggles to overcome racially-motivated oppression, the dreaded loss of a child, workplace discrimination, and threats to his life. He (survived) this all to become an accomplished engineer, the first and only African-American mayor of Lancaster, California, and one of the most well-respected ministers in the history of the Antelope Valley. His life story is amazing and truly inspirational. His story shares lessons of life, love, religion, friends, family, race, and politics. It teaches us the power of forgiveness and explains the strength that is awarded to the forgiver by committing the act of forgiveness so that we can "live better, not bitter."

It has been said that forgiveness is the act of excusing someone else for committing a hurtful or inappropriate act. Forgiveness does not mean forgetting that the act was hurtful or inappropriate, but it does mean rising above the affront and taking strength from your ability to overcome another one of life's inevitable challenges.

Henry Hearns' story contains a lesson for all of us. We are all confronted by hateful and harmful deeds and events at various stages of our life. Take heed, read, and learn what remarkable wonders await us for enduring adversity, exercising the strength to forgive and maintaining a steadfast faith in the almighty.

It gives me great pleasure to encourage others to study the life lessons contained in this marvelous story of faith, forgiveness, and redemption.

HONORABLE HOWARD P. "BUCK" MCKEON (R)
1993–2015 UNITED STATES REPRESENTATIVE,
25TH CONGRESSIONAL DISTRICT CALIFORNIA
FORMER CHAIRMAN, HOUSE ARMED SERVICES COMMITTEE.

# INTRODUCTION

You may not believe this, but I am a white man with an African-American father. While this may be impossible with man, it is possible with God. As I write this [in 2013], it is the 10th anniversary of my birth father's death, a solemn anniversary brightened only by another of equal importance. It was around this same time 10 years ago that Bishop Henry Hearns, an elderly but voracious black preacher from the segregated South, adopted me as his spiritual son.

I first met Henry in the early 1990s, not long after my wife and I moved to Lancaster, California, where Henry was serving as mayor. Because money was tight, we decided to walk to Lancaster Boulevard for the free annual Christmas tree lighting ceremony. When we arrived, there was Mayor Henry Hearns unabashedly preaching Christ's birth to a crowd gathered before him. They had come to see the tree lighting but got to hear the gospel, too. I thought: "Who is this public servant who defies the cry, 'separation of church and state,' to share the good news of our Lord? I must meet this man."

I set out to make him my friend, but as is always the case with Henry, he gave so much more. He bestowed upon me a father-like love and a Father-like grace, as well. For that, I will remain forever grateful.

There are two things that make this deep and unique bond possible: the power and the grace of God. The *power* of God was demonstrated in the breaking of a racial divide that has characterized American life from its inception. The grace of God was so reverently revealed through the heart and life of my spiritual father as he extended forgiveness to those who have so maliciously discriminated against him throughout his long and accomplished life. By choosing to release others from liability, he was able to shield his heart from the piercing arrow of bitterness, keeping him free to love a much younger *white* pastor as a son. Henry has demonstrated with his life the same love and forgiveness shown by Jesus as he was being put to death—*"Father, forgive them for they know not what they do" (Luke 23:34 KJV)*.

I am so thankful for the heroes of the Civil Rights Movement. By exercising their God-given courage standing firm in the face of hatred, these men and women were able to break down seemingly impenetrable racial barriers. Because of that bravery, I have been given the wonderful privilege of having another dad who happens to be black!

As you read my dad's book, my prayer is that you will experience the blessings that come from knowing this wonderful man the way I have. Be inspired by the power of God displayed through his life! There is no limit to what God can do in the life of a person who puts their trust in Him! May you also be challenged to extend grace to others like Henry. If people like Rosa Parks had never sat down on the bus, then perhaps I would have missed out on the privilege of such a rich relationship with Henry. If Christ had never gone to the cross, then the way of forgiveness would not be possible, and bitterness would reign and ruin any hope of sweet fellowship with such a wonderful, spiritual father.

Drink deeply from the spring of Henry Hearns. In him is the living water that comes from Christ.

CHRIS JOHNSON
SR. PASTOR, GRACE CHAPEL
LANCASTER, CALIFORNIA

# PREFACE

### (MAY 31, 2013)

From a very young age I've felt God's mighty hand upon my life. Looking back at my ancestry, both on my mother's side and my father's side, I can see God at work, preparing the way for me to serve Him long before I was born. Only our Lord knows where I'd be without his intervention and guidance. The odds were not in my favor. In fact, many would say the odds of me becoming anything of note were nearly impossible.

The year of my birth—1933—was not a good time to be born black, especially in Mississippi, where blacks were considered by many to be less than livestock. Of course, we've all heard stories about the segregated South, but until you've been on the receiving end of blind prejudice, even hatred, it is difficult to fathom. But it wasn't so much the segregation that inhibited the chances of success for blacks back then, though that hurt, too. It was more the barriers to education, good paying jobs, and civic involvement that threatened to hold down blacks or African Americans, if you prefer.

We were impoverished as a class of people in those days. We were forced to accept low pay for hard labor, usually in the cotton fields. Black children were expected to work the fields as well and many never attended school. I, at least, did all eight years the state allowed. But still, we were essentially illiterate sharecroppers, doing our best to survive as a family. That was our life.

Now, here I sit, gathered with 400 dear friends in the Apollo Ballroom of the Odyssey Restaurant, a grand and beautiful venue in Granada Hills, California, that overlooks the golden lights of the entire San Fernando Valley. I wonder if any of my early past happened at all, if perhaps it was all just a bad dream. There are about 50 round tables draped in white tablecloths and topped with matching china, floral centerpieces, polished silverware sparkling in the amber hue of a dozen or so crystal chandeliers, all atop a hardwood ballroom dance floor. Each table seats eight to ten guests, the men in black ties and the women in elegant gowns and dresses. They're here to mark my 80th birthday. *Eighty.* Wow! I'm breathless because all of this is to celebrate *my* life.

I listen to friend after friend speak, offering up humorous anecdotes and telling the crowd what I've meant to them, to the community, the church and the city for which I served two terms as mayor and 18 years as a city council member. I can't help but reflect upon the things I've experienced, the history I've witnessed, the obstacles I've overcome and the friends of every race I've made. Some of those speaking are dignitaries in their own right—pastors, politicians, business executives, authors, astronauts—yet their words are so kind, so indelible that I'm in awe, not of myself, but of the God who evened the odds enough to give my family and me a chance at a life worth honoring. It wasn't easy getting here, but by His grace and unyielding love, my life has counted for something. God has used me for His glory, and for that, I am so grateful. He blessed me so that I could bless others. He delivered me from the cotton fields and brought me to the glorious Promised Land. God is good!

In a few moments, they will call me up to say a few words. I wish I had the time to share with them all that has happened, but I can't. Even if I had the time, I'm not sure I could hold back the tears long enough to get it all out.

## PREFACE

In the midst of every hardship, God offered up his grace and blessed me through love, marriage and three overlapping careers – pastor, engineer, and politician. He took me to places and positions where few (white or black) were granted access. He allowed me to mentor other people, men, and women, who became leaders and pastors.

I'm just so overcome with joy at the outpouring of love. God has brought me *so very far*.

*—Henry Hearns*

CHAPTER ONE

# BREAKING THE CHAINS

Many of my ancestors were slaves, like most black folks in the early days of our country. My maternal great-grandfather, Andrew Caruthers, was sold twice in the slave market. He died in 1948 at 112, putting his birth in 1836. Slave owners gave him Caruthers as a surname to let the public know to whom he belonged. I lived with my Great-Great Grandpa Caruthers for a time. It was wonderful. He had so much wisdom and insight into those early days of our history, things he passed on to me as a child. He and his mother had been offered on the auction block together but ended up being sold to different families. He remembered that day for the rest of his life, and when he told me about it, I cried. Great-Great Grandpa Caruthers was only about 5 or 6 years old. He grabbed onto his mother's dress, clinging so tightly that he ripped a piece when the two were torn apart. He kept and cherished that piece of his mother's dress for the rest of his life. Sadly, he never saw her again.

I personally knew my Great Granddaddy Lump Hearn (the "s" was added to the end of our name later) (on my father's side as well). White folks purchased his mother on the slave market and had probably engaged sexually with her. That's our suspicion anyway because Grandpa Lump was a very light-skin baby. At some point, the white family that owned

Lump set him free, giving him 300 acres to farm and make a living. That land got passed down to his son, Granddaddy Percy Hearn.

Now, you could not tell Percy from a white man to save your life—blonde hair, blue eyes, white skin. In fact, he told me many times about when he had boarded the train in Byhalia, Mississippi, or in Memphis, Tennessee, and had been forced to sit in the white section because the ticket people thought he was white! He always wanted to sit in the black section, but the ticket punchers insisted Granddaddy Percy was fibbing when he said he was black, not white. They'd tell him, "No. You can't sit there. You need to sit where you belong in the white section." I remember walking with him sometimes along the Byhalia country roads, and Grandpa Percy would tell me these stories, and we'd laugh together. A Negro looking white was certainly odd, but back then, it had its privileges for obvious reasons.

Mother's side of the family had been very poor, but those 300 acres made Daddy's side rich. I used to walk to Sunday school down a gravel road with Great-Grandpa Lump, going to the Methodist Church in Byhalia. He'd take us to Sunday school, telling us as we walked about how it used to be, how we had it good with the white folks because they had cared enough about our family to give us that land. I'm getting emotional just thinking about that. Wow! Imagine that, and it was so long ago. Some of that land is owned by our family in Byhalia today. A few in the family got in a fight over it some time ago. I don't know how it turned out, but all that land and the old house were all there when I came along, though I'd been born elsewhere.

My parents had both worked for white folks in some capacity or another for much of my young life, whether it was sharecropping the cotton fields, cooking and cleaning their houses, or driving for them. But in just about every instance, God had blessed our family with compassionate employers. Racism was alive and well in 1930s Mississippi, and we experienced our share. But God opened doors for us that had been closed to most Southern blacks. God showed us He was true to His holy word and that if we walked uprightly, He would sustain us. The more God sustained us, the more we held to our faith. We had faith in a Lord that delivers, in a God who protects, in a Father who loves, and in a Son who took the sin of the world upon Himself for our sakes. Through it all, we learned to be gracious, just as our Lord Jesus was gracious when persecuted. He harbored no malice, uttered no defiling word in response to the abuse He endured, and made no gesture other than complete submission to the will of He who sent Him. We tried to do the same.

It wasn't easy, but my parents saved and eventually bought their own farm. Their oldest boy, Henry Wyatt Hearn (that's me), would go on from the cotton fields of Mississippi to serve honorably in the Korean War, earn multiple college degrees when most colleges were inaccessible to blacks, train to become a civil engineer and then work at an Air Force base, get elected as the first African-American city council member, served two terms as mayor of a medium-size city, and then honored as bishop of a wonderful church. This all happened because God laid His mighty hand upon my life early. No good thing would have come my way by erecting a wall of bitterness, which is so common in the hearts of the persecuted. King David said it best: *"For the Lord God is a sun and shield; The Lord will give grace and glory; no good thing will He withhold from those who walk uprightly."* Psalm 84:11 (ESV)

By keeping my eyes focused upward, I've been able to walk uprightly in the Lord. God has anointed me with the oil of gladness. He has put the sweet salve of graciousness on my lips—and it tastes so good!

CHAPTER TWO

# NO CIRCUMSTANCE SO GREAT

## MAMA

Though the land and house on Daddy's side were still there, I was born elsewhere—in the cook's house on the McCrary Plantation in Byhalia, Mississippi. Mother's real name was

Birdie, but she went by "Bertha." She had married once before marrying my father, moving with her former husband to work the plantation. Shortly thereafter, Mama and her first husband divorced. He left, but Thomas Ingram and Ada Dee McCrary asked my mother to stay. A few months later, my mother met my father, Earnest Hearn, and married him sometime before I was born. They'd gotten ahead of themselves with their intimacy, but Daddy did the right thing and married Mother after getting her pregnant. Although my father's name was Earnest, everybody called him "Red," a common term used for lighter-skinned Negroes.

The McCrary Plantation blanketed a beautiful piece of rolling landscape that was about 75 acres in all, with a great big white house on the largest hilltop, nestled in the shade of a few giant oaks. The cook's house, where my parents lived, was just off the back of the main residence, slightly down the hill. That's where I was born in a little old cottage-like house with no indoor plumbing or electricity. We had an outhouse, of course, and a spigot of the main house where we got our water. We used kerosene lamps that gave off lots of light when needed. But it was humble living and certainly not the place to give birth. Still, back then, segregation forced most black mothers-to-be to give birth at home.

Our diminutive home had just two bedrooms, a common living area, and a kitchen where we also washed clothes with a tub and washboard. We took baths in that *same* washtub! My parents would heat the water on our wood stove, pour it into the tub until the water temperature turned just right, and then we would all bathe, one at a time, sharing the same water. We did the same thing everywhere we lived growing up; and when my siblings came along, the girls would get to bathe first in the cleanest and warmest water, the boys thereafter in whatever water remained. We never changed the water until everybody had finished bathing because water was scarce for blacks.

Mama was a pretty little dark woman with a wonderful disposition and many great qualities. She looked Native American, or so people said. Mama could get her hair wet in the rain or wash it and it didn't curl at all. Her black hair was so beautiful, along with her earthy yet pretty features, that she became the envy of many other black women.

Among her great qualities was the ability to cook. People just loved Mama's cooking! She could make just about any meal out of potatoes, from potato pancakes to boiled potatoes with a little meat in them to anything. It always tasted good. She could have made dirt taste good!

She also knew how to get along with people. Mama had a way of embedding herself into the hearts of all who knew her, even white folks. They loved her because no matter what happened, no matter how badly she was treated, she responded graciously. I've tried to emulate Mama my entire life.

I remember Mama telling me that while carrying me, Mrs. McCrary thought she might be having twins because her belly was so huge. Mrs. McCrary told her, "Bertha, you need to be careful. You're cooking for us, and you make such great food, but you really need to take it easy. We'll be all right."

Mama was so small, too tiny to be carrying such a large baby in her belly. But Mrs. McCrary was a firm believer in our Lord Jesus Christ also and would pray over my mother. I think her love for Mama stemmed partly from that belief, even though both lived in a time and area of extreme prejudice against blacks. It just goes to show that what the Apostle Paul said in 1 Corinthians 13:13 (NKJV) is true, *"And now abide faith, hope, love, these three; but the greatest of these is love."* Love can indeed conquer all. Love breaks down barriers. Love heals. Love restores. Love gives life to unlikely relationships.

Mrs. McCrary loved my mother so much that she refused to bring in a midwife, which was standard in those days, preferring instead to have her own personal physician, Dr. Senter, see to Mama. Although Dr. Senter was white, he agreed to Mrs. McCrary's request. She had money and wasn't worried about the cost, after all. She just wanted to make sure my mother survived giving birth to me.

On the morning of April 23, 1933, when my delivery seemed imminent, Dr. Senter came to my parents' house black medical bag in hand, ready to do his business. Mother and Father had a big, wooden eating table there at the house and that's where Dr. Senter arranged her. There on that sturdy, multi-purpose table, under the white-hot glow of a few hanging kerosene lamps, a cool breeze passing through the torn, front door screen and settling on Mama's sweaty brow like a comforting hand from God, Mama labored to deliver her firstborn. The doctor, however, quickly discovered I was too big for my petite mother to deliver without risking her own life. In his mind, the only viable option was to cut me into pieces in her womb and then remove me. They didn't have C-sections back then, at least not for black folks, so the only way to save my mother's life, in Dr. Senter's experience, was to kill me! But God intervened just as the doctor got ready to begin. It had to be God because the timing was perfect.

Before Dr. Senter could start the procedure, there came a knock at the door. It was a Dr. Moore, a colleague of his, who had dropped by the house to see if Dr. Senter could help him with one of his patients. The way my mother told it, Dr. Senter said to Dr. Moore, "As soon as I cut this baby out so we don't lose Bertha, I'll come and help you." Mama said she could hear this conversation going on around her as she lay there, praying all the while. Well, Dr. Moore took a look at Mama and said to Dr. Senter, "Would you mind if I try to deliver this baby? Let me work with this awhile before you proceed."

So Dr. Moore told my mother what to do and when to push, and lo and behold, I was born—and in one piece, thank the Lord!

When Mama told me that story about how I was almost aborted, well, I had to praise God for Dr. Moore. Had he not given me Moore time, I would not be here today. I'm still in awe that my tiny little mother could deliver a baby weighing 13 pounds and 14 ounces. Only by the mighty hand of God did we both survive!

Now, you might be wondering where my father was during this critical time. The way I understand it, my father wanted to be there for my birth, and he, too, was concerned that my mother might not live through the delivery of such a large baby. His employer, Dr. McAuley, didn't think the birth of Daddy's first child or the threat to his wife's life warranted time off from his duties as the doctor's personal driver. Some men might have quit over such an offense, but not my father. He and Mama would need his income after my birth, just as they had before it. In Daddy's mind, the scarcity of secure employment for blacks back then left him no other option but to go to work that day. He could not risk losing his job.

It was still a different situation at the McCary's. Mama said that after I was born, Mrs. McCrary put on a grand celebration, inviting all of my mother's friends and family. Mrs. McCrary was just as proud of my mother and me as she would have been of her own daughter and grandchild. She doted over me, too—a little black baby. Just loved me! Mrs. McCrary made Mama take it easy when she returned to work. That's what I mean when I say we had it differently than other blacks back then. The other people working on farms would be back working the fields again, picking cotton or whatever, just days after having their babies. Mrs. McCrary treated my mother sometimes as if she were another white woman. Mama said that just didn't happen in the days of old. Whites would rarely treat blacks as equals. I'll never forget how fondly my mother recalled Mrs. McCrary. Later, after we had moved to the McAuley Plantation in Byhalia, Mrs. McCrary would bring us food because she was concerned we weren't eating well enough.

Mr. McCrary also used to dote on me. He owned a dry goods store downtown where people bought feed, clothing tools, and other things (that was in addition to his plantation) and would give me some type of birthday present every year. It could be a ball cap, an article of clothing, or some other item from his store. Sometimes he'd even let me pick what gift I wanted. Mr. and Mrs. McCrary were wonderful people. Their love for us helped stem any hatred for whites that I might have had otherwise.

Mama was a very positive, praying woman, which was one of the reasons people liked her so much. Her belief in our Lord was so strong! So strong! Her father, Earnest (E.H.) Garmond, my granddaddy on her side, was one of the presiding elders of the Methodist Church, having fathered many churches—a wonderful man of God. He died at 100 years old in

1978. Before passing, he gave me all the information on his life so I could do the eulogy at his funeral, which I was honored to give.

Mama's deep faith had a profound effect on me, not only as a child in racially charged Mississippi but later in life as well. She could read a little but had never been to school. Mama would get people to read the Bible to her, especially Mr. George Poole, the man who taught eighth grade. He would come to the house and read the Bible for all of us. Mama would listen, following along in her own Bible, and then might say, "Okay now, read a little slower so I can keep up with you."

She learned to read that way and to write that way. She was just a terrific woman and very smart about things.

## DADDY

One of the more amusing memories I have of my father had to do with his nickname. When we were poor sharecroppers, the locals called Daddy "Red." Later, after my father and mother bought their own land and had big money coming in, at least for those days, people started calling Daddy "*Big* Red." That always makes me chuckle when I think about it. I look a lot like my father, and that warms my heart when I think about it. I loved him dearly.

My father drove for Dr. McAuley, who soon insisted Mama come work for him as well on his plantation. It was a sad day for Mama and me when Daddy moved us from the McCrary's to the McAuley's, just behind the white people's cemetery. I couldn't have been but 4 or 5 years of age, but I remember being upset about leaving the family who had cared so much for us. I owed my very life to Mrs. McCrary, after all. The good thing, though, was that the McAuley Plantation was only about a mile-and-a-half as the crow flies from the McCrary Plantation, close enough for us to continue our relationship with the Ada Dee and Ingram McCrary.

It was on the McAuley Plantation that we began sharecropping cotton, which is where the owner of the crop pays the pickers by giving them a meager share, which would then be sold for cash. Daddy still drove for Dr. McAuley, though, leaving the picking to the rest of us.

As a young man, Daddy was a womanizer and a confused soul. He was not saved, then. I was about 12 years old when he did give his life to the Lord. His whole life changed after that. It was an amazing transformation, a true testament to the power of the Holy Spirit in a person's life. Daddy became more serious about his responsibilities, working harder and saving whatever money he could to give us a better life later. He came to love my mother *tremendously*. They had their share of arguments—one that may have gotten physical if I remember correctly—but they loved each other with their whole hearts. Nobody could ever deny that.

Like most young men in the 1940s, my father got drafted into the Army. World War II had begun, and though they needed soldiers who could fight, most blacks served in the rear echelons. My father was no different. He was drafted but never left the states. When my father returned from the Army, he began working long hours at Chicago and Southern Airlines. Daddy stood about 5'11" tall, a few inches shorter than me, and he had great strength. He was a wonderful father, spending as much time as he could with us and always telling some kind of joke to make us laugh. On Saturday evenings, after we had purchased our own farm where we worked five-and-a-half days per week, Daddy would break out a charcoal bucket, heat it up and we'd have ourselves a fish-fry—just my mother and father and us kids. They were a very special part of my life until their passing. We'd fry up some catfish caught in Coldwater Creek, not far from the house. Daddy would set his hooks out at night and sometimes would snag 30- and 40-pound fish. He would then fillet those fish and cook them in his charcoal bucket. You haven't tasted fish until you've had them out of a charcoal bucket! If they had charcoal buckets during Jesus' time, He would have fired up a few buckets to fry all that fish He fed the multitudes.

Jesus and the apostles knew the bonds created by breaking bread together, the act of sitting down with others to enjoy a meal and fellowship. A meal together can help ease anxieties in our homes, bringing families closer together, which is something this virtual world so desperately needs. As families, we have become more detached from one another through technology rather than closer together. Oh, we may text each other a lot, but how much face-to-face fellowship and heartfelt touching have we lost with loved ones because of the convenience of texting? Texting even happens with one another while at home together! The result is more discord within the family and less grace, more selfishness and less selflessness, more rebellion and less unity. No matter how great you think, smart phone technology is, a text will never replace a loving kiss in greeting, nor a tender touch when another is hurting.

I'll always admire my parents for their commitment to spending time with us kids, for their affection, their active participation in our lives, and for their generous love. I wish more children could experience that type of parenting. The world certainly would be a better place to live. They never let their circumstances or anything else get in the way of *family time*.

CHAPTER THREE

# FINDING JOY IN POVERTY

I think the biggest thing for me as a child growing up in Mississippi was going to church. In the summer, our church would have revival after revival coming through, so the church became a daily activity some weeks if we didn't have to work on the farm, of course. Most of the other kids were there, so it was fun, and I enjoyed the services. I loved the singing! Oh, how the church came alive with singing!

Trying to find out what the Bible had to say: God kept my mind occupied. At the time, I could not fathom the idea of an invisible person —one I couldn't touch or see—loving me and wanting me *so much* that He sacrificed His Son upon a cross. I would sit and talk to the deacons and other churchgoers, trying to understand all I could about my invisible God. What I discovered over time was that Jesus' willing sacrifice upon the cross and the Father's *willing* sacrifice of His Son so He could have a right relationship with me was the ultimate display of godly grace. Even from the cross, Jesus pleaded with God to have mercy on his killers, saying, *"Father, forgive them, for they do not know what they do."* (Luke 23:34 KJV) This would become an example for me to follow for the rest of my days. If Jesus could forgive those putting Him to death, surely I could forgive any offense against me because nothing could ever compare.

Churches didn't have air conditioning back then either, and in the South, with its humidity, it could get awfully hot inside. But those old-time churches were built with windows that you could raise. The deacons and elders would lift those windows in such a way as to get the best draft coming through. It could still get hot, and you'd find a lot of people fanning themselves with paper or the open palm of a hand. Mostly, though, we just sweated it out, thankful to the Lord that we had a church to go to, filling the place with "Amens!" and "Hallelujahs!"

Rev. Hibler was the pastor at the New Zion Baptist Church, the same place we attended school during the week. It's still there today. Each year, I go back to Byhalia to visit all these places. My first school teacher's name was Cassie Johnson. After that came George and Mattie Pool, who were a sister and brother team. But since blacks were allowed to attend only until the eighth grade, our teachers, being black also, didn't have a lot of formal schooling either. Cassie had attended Mississippi Industrial College, a private church school up in Holly Springs, Mississippi. She knew more about the history of people like George Washington Carver. Before Cassie, we didn't get those kinds of lessons because the white folks wouldn't give us that information.

In fact, the schoolbooks we used were the leftover or used schoolbooks of the white kids at the "whites only" schools. There were no black heroes or historical figures discussed in those pages, only white. The white children knew that the black kids would be getting their old books. Sometimes we'd pick up a book with the word "nigger" written inside in large letters or messages like, "Hope you enjoy this, nigger. You can't learn, no way."

Those things used to make me so angry and sometimes I would catch myself thinking, "When I get old enough, I'm going to pay some people back." But the Lord did a number on my mind, always reminding me of Mrs. McCrary and how much that white woman loved my mother and me. Surely, not all whites were bad, I would conclude.

Jesus also faced harmful bigotry, but the Bible tells us, *"When they hurled their insults at Him, He did not retaliate; when He suffered, He made no threats. Instead, He entrusted Himself to Him who judges justly."* (1 Peter 2:23 NIV) Once again, Jesus chose grace—free, *unmerited* favor—rather than condemnation and judgment. He had every right to be angry and bitter toward His malicious and violent accusers, just as you and I may have against ours, but Jesus sacrificed that right, opting instead for grace— *always grace*.

Many of the white kids had dogs and cats as pets, but my pets growing up were the farm animals—the cows, calves, horses, and others. We had 10 cows on the McAuley place. We owned them. I milked each cow twice a day, and spending so much time with them kind of made the cows feel like friends. But if I had anything close to a pet growing up, it was this old hog we had around the farm—a big and smelly, snorting but lovable beast. He never had to be corralled; he just roamed about freely. Some days, while I was out picking cotton or working the fields, I'd take a break under an old oak tree, and that old hog would come and lie there with me. I would lie back with my head against his fat belly, arms behind my head, just daydreaming in the shade. He wouldn't move. The funniest thing, really, is a black boy and his pet hog! It might have made a great Norman Rockwell painting!

Mama didn't make much money. She got maybe a dollar per week cash payment in addition to the cook's residence if I remember correctly. She had to be resourceful. We had very little money for clothing, so Mama would take the cloth sacks that the animal feed came in and would stitch up some shirts and britches for us kids. She would take those sacks and wash them in homemade lye soap wash. Mama made the soap by boiling the meat skins from the pork with lye and something else (I don't remember the other ingredient). The strong soap stripped the lettering off the feed sacks. The sacks cleaned up nicely. Then Mama would use an old pedaling-type sewing machine to make us shirts and pants.

Or if she had to, in those colder years, Mama might get me some hand-me-downs from the white folks. I had shoes, but I had to take care of them because I owned one pair at a time. That's one of the reasons we'd run around barefoot whenever possible. Mama wanted us to save our shoes for colder days and special occasions. This is one of the oldest photos I have of me wearing clothes that Mama made out of sackcloth.

When I think back on those restrictions in comparison to today's youth, even the poor in our country, I'm reminded of the blessings God has bestowed upon these United States, only to be hidden by a growing sense of entitlement. One of the things God's word teaches is that there is great benefit in suffering, something we Americans, particularly the latest generation, seem to have forgotten.

The apostle Paul teaches us in Romans 5:3-5 (NIV): *"Not only so, but we also glory in our sufferings, because we know that suffering produces perseverance; perseverance, character; and character, hope. And hope does not put us to shame because God's love has been poured out into our hearts through the Holy Spirit, who has been given to us."*

We killed or grew most of what we ate in those days. Hunting rabbits was a big deal in my childhood. Funny thing is, not all of us had shotguns. Some kids, like me, only had a "tap stick." Now, a tap stick was a small tree branch about two or three feet long. On the end of mine I'd tie a large steel nut, the type that comes off a big machine and easily found in the junkyard. I would throw that tap stick at the rabbit. I got to where I could lead the rabbit like a quarterback leads a receiver with a pass. I'd watch the rabbit, guess which way he would break, and then hurl my tap stick ahead of him, timing it to where it'd hit the rabbit and knock it out and kill it right on the spot! That big nut would give the stick accuracy and momentum, like a spear or an arrow, giving those rabbits little chance for survival when it struck.

A normal meal for us back then would be something with potatoes, some black-eyed peas, whippoorwill peas, greens, cabbage, and other vegetables.

Wherever we moved, we would have a garden where Mama would plant vegetables of all sorts. Our largest garden was on the Rivers Burks Plantation.

During the winter months, we had bags and bags of peanuts, popcorn, dried peas, and other dried goods we could eat by the fire. We'd harvest our red potatoes and take them to Johnnie Taylor, who owned a "potato kiln" not far from our Byhalia home. Again, I'm getting emotional thinking back on it because I remember loading up our potatoes in the wagon and taking them up to the potato kiln with my daddy. Taylor would take our potatoes, keeping about 20 percent of them for his pay, and then put them in his kiln to help preserve them against the frost and cold. The kiln, which was a big wooden building built partly underground, had a heater inside to help keep the crops warm. They'd turn a little yellow, but they wouldn't get frostbitten. That's how we preserved all our vegetables. We'd go up from time to time, get some potatoes and greens from our stock, and together with some pork, we'd have us a good winter meal. Daddy and me riding up to Taylor's with a wagonload of potatoes is a special memory. One of the things I attribute to my good health today is eating right all my life, even in those tough times. Praise be to God for His blessings!

As I've alluded, I was not the only child in the Hearn household. Two years after my birth, my sister Birdie May entered our fold. We were always close. Even today, we talk almost every day. Despite our closeness, Birdie and I would argue about everything. The issue didn't matter; we liked to take opposing views for the sake of it. I remember how thin she was growing up and how I would start in on her by calling her "Olive Oil" after Popeye's pencil-thin girlfriend. Oh, she just hated that! Birdie would retaliate by calling me "fat and lazy," a reference to some well-known sloth in town. We'd laugh about it later, so there was no love lost between us. We were just being siblings.

A year after Birdie, my other sister Laura was born. You talk about a talent! Laura just had a beautiful voice. When she and Mama got to singing in the fields, the day just flew by. It was like we hadn't a care in the world. In truth, we could all sing and later, when we became teenagers, we would form a singing group called *The Family Five*.

My brother Douglas arrived next, followed by my youngest brother, James Monroe, who would be the first of my siblings to pass on into heaven. In the following photograph, you can see Mama holding Douglas, Great-Great Grandpa Caruthers (a former slave), me (left), Birdie (right), and Laura. James Monroe was yet to be born. This photo would have been taken sometime around 1938 or 1939 on the McAuley Plantation, I believe.

This photograph shows me (right) with my brothers Douglas (middle) and James (left):

I just loved growing up with my brothers and sisters. Love them still today. They have been the most supportive siblings imaginable, and I praise God for gifting them to me. But they could be mischievous, as well, especially in their youth.

I remember a time when my parents were away. Being the oldest of the five kids, Mama put me in charge. Of course, I may have let that go to my head a bit. Well, my brothers and sisters thought they would straighten me out once I fell asleep in my favorite spot, a chair on the front porch of our rickety house. Now, remember I said we seldom wore shoes? I had fallen asleep in that chair with my bare feet stretched out and crossed like I was some sort of king or something. That was all the opportunity my brothers and sisters needed. They took a few small scraps of paper, slipped them between my toes, and then lit them with a match. When that flame hit my skin, wow! I jumped so high that I just about hit the porch roof. Well, that was just the funniest thing to Birdie, Laura, Douglas, and James, but I didn't laugh. In fact, I chased them in every direction as they tried to run and laugh at the same time. Today, that sort of thing might get some kids arrested, but back then, a "hot foot" was a common prank. Even now, as I think back on it, I have to chuckle. But it really could have had some terrible consequences. Please don't ever try it. Just laugh at my experience and let it go.

CHAPTER FOUR

# A NEW PLANTATION— A NEW SEASON IN MY LIFE

I'll never forget the first time I looked at Dr. McAuley's car. Daddy still drove for the doctor, but I'd never had occasion to see the car. One day my father slipped away from Dr. McAuley's office without permission and had come home to retrieve something he'd forgotten to take to work. He parked on the slope leading up to the house. Now, even at a young age, anything mechanical fascinated me. When I caught sight of that beautiful wine-colored Mercury, well, I just had to know how it worked. I climbed inside while Daddy was off getting what he had come home to get. Having that car all to myself to explore sent me over the moon with joy. I started pressing this button and that one, looking to see what each did when engaged. Then I saw the keys still in the ignition. *Man! Really?* I started teasing those keys with my fingertips. *Sure do feel cool to the touch, these keys. Wonder what she sounds like. No*, I thought, *I'd better not. Daddy will bust my hide*! I looked about and when I didn't see Daddy anywhere near, I fired that hot rod up. Oh, I am telling you! The way that engine purred, that hollow *pop* of the exhaust when I removed my foot from the gas pedal to let the engine de-rev. It sounded like the voice of the

Almighty to my little ears! God Himself couldn't have sounded any prettier.

Well, somehow, during that experience, I accidentally released the parking-brake. I didn't know much about whether a car was in gear or out of gear, but Daddy had obviously left Dr. McAuley's beautiful car in neutral. It took a second before that car got to rolling backward, picking up speed something quick! I couldn't figure out how to stop it, but that Mercury stopped eventually—when it slammed backward into a tree farther down the slope! I don't remember what Dr. McAuley did to my father over that incident, but I know Daddy tore my hind end up big time! I couldn't have been but 5 or 6 years old when it happened, but that same dogged curiosity has followed me throughout my entire life. I suppose it's the reason I became an engineer.

Old man McAuley, as I used to call him (behind his back, of course), had to be about 65 years old when we first moved to his farm. He had a son named Deaton and two daughters, Gene and Bonnie. Deaton, who was about my father's age, had a son named Malcolm, who was close to my age. My parents would send me to town for things once I got big enough to work around the farm. I passed by Deaton's house often. I'll never forget this one time when Malcolm had left his new toy truck outside in the yard. I loved that bright-yellow Tonka truck the minute I saw it. I snatched it up and took it over to my house to play.

I didn't have much in the way of toys, but I usually made do with what I could find. I'd go to the junk pile near our house, scour the heap for discarded or broken toys, and then take them home. I'd work those toys back into shape, just as if they were new.

Not this time, and as fate would have it, Mama saw me playing with that toy truck and wanted to know where I'd gotten it. I said from the junkyard up the road. It was a bold-faced lie, of course, but Mama seemed satisfied with my answer and went back into the house. I thought: *That was easy*. But my mother was sharp. She recognized that the truck looked too nice to have come from the junkyard. She came back out and asked, "Boy, where'd you get that truck? Honest now."

Dropping my head, I told her I had stolen the truck from little Malcolm. Mama tore a switch from a nearby tree and used it to march me all the way through town with little Malcolm's toy truck in my hands back to Deaton McAuley's house. Deaton's place was about a mile-and-half walk from the graveyard where I was playing. I had plenty of time to work up a fright over what would happen when we arrived. I knew my mother meant business with that switch. It was just a matter of time before she switched it on my backside.

When we got to the back door, Mama made me knock. We waited, and when Deaton brought little Malcolm to the door, Mama made me ask Malcolm to forgive me. He said it was all right, and I handed him the Tonka truck. Mama didn't think it was all right. After we returned home, she sure enough showed me what that switch was for! I'll never forget that beating. Mama may have been tiny, but she took big swings!

Mama was a very industrious woman and very sharp in her thinking. When my father got saved and wanted to change his life, he started listening to her more, particularly about saving money. Mama's convictions came straight from the Lord, and my father was no fool. He could see she was an honest woman, and if God had made her that way, he wanted some of God, too. If God wanted him to provide for his family, then he was going to provide a better life than the one we had at the time. With Mama's help, Daddy started saving for our own farm.

It was while we lived on Dr. McAuley's plantation that we first started sharecropping. That old shack we lived in was just as fragile as glass. One tap in the wrong place, and it would have surely crumbled to the ground. I would have to say that our house on McAuley's place, seen in the photograph below, was the worst dump we ever lived in. The beams were rickety, old, dry-rotted wood held up by termite-infested studs. Probably wasn't a true right angle in that entire house. Still, we were grateful for a roof over our heads and food to eat.

Now, Dr. McAuley and some of the other rich white men ran the Draft Board in Byhalia. They could have anybody they wanted put into the military and anybody they wanted kept out. Dr. McAuley saw a change in my father. No longer just driving the car and saying, "Yes'a, boss," but saying, "Yes'a boss," while putting a little money aside to buy his own farm. Dr. McAuley had my father put into the military, quite possibly because he, like a lot of whites back then, didn't believe blacks had a right to anything other than their daily bread. Rather than seeing us become land owners like him, Dr. McAuley saw it best to split apart our family, having Daddy drafted and sent away. That was during WWII when I was about 8 years old.

Once Daddy left home for the Army, Dr. McAuley put us out and told us we had to find another place to live. Mama moved us to the Rivers Burks Plantation. J. Rivers Burks owned a café and supermarket in downtown Byhalia. He was a rich, white man who liked to work in the kitchen of his café with all his black cooks. That just didn't happen back then. Well, Mama went to the back door of that café one day, knocked, and asked one of the black cooks to get Mr. Burks. When Mr. Burks came to the rear door of his café, Mama said, "My name is Bertha. This is my son, Henry. He can plow and work the farm as good as any man."

Wow! I can't believe how emotional I'm getting thinking about this! She said, "Dr. McAuley has put us out. He told us we have to move now that my husband is in the Army. Says I don't have enough children of age to pick enough cotton, so he's putting us out. We need a home. We'll do anything you want. I'll take care of your house and cook for you. I'm a real good cook, Mr. Burks. And though my kids are young, we can raise a few acres of cotton for you if you'll just give us a home."

## A New Plantation—A New Season in My Life

Mama went to Rivers Burks because she had heard from others working the plantation that Mr. Burks, just like Mrs. McCrary, cared about people, even black people.

He said, "All right. You say your name is Bertha?"

Mama said, "Yes, sir, and I got four other kids besides this one. This is my oldest, Henry."

Mr. Burks said, "I'll send a truck to pick up you and your things move you to my farm."

That's what he did. But I led my cows by foot the seven miles from McAuley to Rivers Burks. Now, by then, we had eaten that pet hog of mine, so I didn't have to worry about him. But I walked those 10 cows right through downtown Byhalia, all on my own. Probably looked a little funny, but I did it.

Once at the Rivers Burks Plantation, I learned how to operate all kinds of farm equipment: combines, hay balers, and plowing mules. Mr. Burks really took an interest in me. I think he saw in me a willingness to learn the machines and to work hard for him. In return, he dedicated time to teaching me. Once again, God had shown us a favor because later on, when we bought our own farm, I was able to use what I'd learned from Mr. Burks to help make our farm productive. What Dr. McAuley intended for bad by having my father drafted, God intended for good. I'll elaborate on this later, but it's a story very similar to Joseph and his brothers, with a very similar result!

After we moved from the McAuley place, a terrible thing happened to me that would impact my relationships with girls well into my adulthood. When we walked home from school, some of us would cut through a pasture as a shortcut. Others would walk around, going the way they had to go to get to their respective houses. For me, cutting through that pasture trimmed a good mile of walking off of my trek home, so that's the way I usually went. Well, one day, I was cutting through the pasture with two 14-year-old girls who went to school with me. (We only had one schoolhouse for all the black children, no matter the grade.) We got just beyond a fence when the two girls asked me if I knew what a girl's privates looked like. It embarrassed me, and I didn't answer. I was only 8 or 9 years old, after all. Then they went on to ask if I would let them see *my* privates. I said, "No!" But they dropped their books and started wrestling me to the ground in the pasture. They were too strong for me, and got my pants open. I don't want to get into exact details, but after it was all over, they stood over me and told me that if I told anybody about what they'd done to me that, they would have me beaten up by "Bootsie," one of the bigger bullies from school.

Years passed before I told my mother about it. I had never told a soul until the day I mentioned it to Mama. She hugged me and cried over me, asking why I hadn't told her when it happened. I stayed away from those girls after the molestation. If it looked like we would be heading through that pasture at the same time, I would make sure to run ahead or go the long way around. Why those two girls did that to me I'll never truly know. Perhaps they, too, were molested by somebody at one time or another. All I really know is that this incident traumatized me and affected my relationships with girls for a very long time, even with my wife, whom I met when I was 16 years old.

This sort of incident demonstrates the worst in mankind. It is not the fault of God for allowing this wretched behavior to happen, but the fault of man—of sin entering into man and woman in the Garden of Eden. We are sick right down to our souls. The only remedy is to die to ourselves, to completely forsake our right of claim to anything, including our own bodies. Instead, let Christ, the living Word of God and the salvation of mankind, take His rightful place on the ship that is our life. Give Him the helm and full control of the rudder and canvas.

What happened to me is not unlike what happened to Jesus, innocent and powerless on that cross against such unthinkable abuse, to the point of death to His physical body. For me, however, powerless to atrocious abuse as well, there was the death of my innocence. The great thing is that we are not alone in such experiences. God, who gave His Son for us out of tremendous love, suffers through the hurt right along with us. He is no different than any other loving Father who comes alongside his beloved child when they're hurting, our loving Father's heart aching for us as He offers comfort.

This chapter brings to mind a very important lesson that's as relevant today as it was for people back then. Many of us have had humble and difficult beginnings. Some are going through trials even as I write these words. But we cannot allow difficulties to embitter us. We must learn to proclaim in all circumstances: *"Praise the Lord! Oh, give thanks to the Lord, for He is good! For His mercy endures forever."* (Psalm 106:1 NKJV)

I've learned in my 82 years that how we respond to our circumstances affects our attitude toward other people. Bitterness leads to *me*-thinking and not *He*-thinking and a self-centeredness destined to disappoint everybody. Hardship does not equal defeat. Hardship allows the Lord to deliver us and to remind us that though this world may bring us trouble, He has overcome the world. God is bigger than any circumstance we might have been born into, more powerful than any force wanting to hold us back. Through prayer, trust, and with the same grace shown us by Jesus on the cross, we can rise from the ashes to be used for His glory— *each and every one of us.*

CHAPTER FIVE

# OVERCOMING RACIAL TENSION

We *are saying that we are determined to be men. We are determined to be people. We are saying that we are God's children [too]."—* Dr. Martin Luther King Jr. (From his speech, *I've Been to the Mountaintop*, delivered at Mason Temple in Memphis, Tennessee, April 3, 1968, just one day before his assassination)

Mississippi race relations during the 1930s, 40s, and 50s can only be described as a brewing tempest, finally unleashing its fury in 1962 when a young black man named James Meredith chose to attend the University of Mississippi, forcing 1954's Brown vs. The Board of Education into the public consciousness. Meredith's first days on campus required hundreds of U.S. Marshalls and support from thousands from the Army National Guard, called out by Attorney General Robert Kennedy. Dozens of marshals were injured, and two people were killed over the course of several weeks as those there to keep Meredith safe clashed with whites bent on maintaining the status quo. It was a test of President Kennedy's commitment to equal rights for all.

Before the Civil Rights Movement, blacks living in Mississippi faced persecution of every kind. When we lived on the McAuley Plantation,

Mama wanted to buy me a new pair of shoes for Easter. But she couldn't just go out and buy them. She had to get permission from Dr. McAuley, even though we were supposedly free people. That's the way it was for all us black sharecroppers. If a black sharecropper needed shoes or, clothing, or anything else for survival, they had to go to the white plantation owner and ask for money. If the plantation owner approved, he would then give them a ticket against a share of their crop of cotton or whatever else they were picking. That's how we got money to buy things.

When I was young, I can remember Daddy going up to the white man's house wherever we were, removing his cap and holding it in his hands, laughing at things being said that weren't really that amusing. Daddy never had any interaction with Mr. McCrary, so that did not happen there. This sort of thing happened regularly at the McAuley plantation, and also at some of the dry goods stores and gas stations around. My Daddy had a word he would use when talking to the white folks—"Cap'n." He'd say, "Hey, Cap'n! Hey, Cap'n!" Then he'd let out a "Ha, ha, ha! Cap'n, you're a wonderful guy. Yes, sir!"

I can remember walking down the streets of Byhalia and if a white person was approaching, we'd have to get off the sidewalk or street and let them pass. Only when they were a good way off from us could we continue on our way again. I can remember also when a little white boy named Herbert, who was a couple of years older, used to play with me. Herbert came to me when he turned 13 saying, "Henry, don't you think it's about time you started saying 'Yes, sir' and 'No, sir' to me?"

I told him, "I'll tell you what, Herbert. If you say 'Yes, sir' and 'No, sir' to me, I'll say the same to you."

That was the end of my friendship with Herbert. He ran home to tell his daddy what I'd said. I never heard another thing about it.

Many of the southern black folks lived in fear of the whites, but we didn't. We had no reason to live in fear because we did what we were supposed to do. We were definitely obedient. We had to be. I remember rolling up to the gas pumps to fill up the car. It didn't matter how far along we might be in filling up our car, if a white person pulled in with their car, we had to immediately stop and pull around to the back of the line. Sometimes, we would be there for hours just trying to fill up our car! But like Mrs. McCrary and Mr. Burks, there were those whites who treated us better, who somehow saw the injustice in all that nonsense. They'd pull into the station, and as we got set to back out or pull around behind them, would tell us, "No. Go ahead and fill your tank. It's all right."

Daddy would say, "No, sir. I know I'm supposed . . ."

But they'd interrupt, "No, boy. You go ahead and get your gas."

We didn't live in fear because we didn't give any reason for anything bad to happen to us. We were courteous and obedient—overly courteous.

My family, once again, got the benefit of being treated a little better than other blacks, partly because we were lighter-skinned and partly because the Hearn family owned land on my daddy's side. We who had lighter skin were considered to be in a different class than darker-skinned Negroes. Nevertheless, we knew our place. If I boarded a bus to travel to Memphis or somewhere else, even if there were no white people on the bus, I had to go to the back. It did not matter how many blacks were on the bus. The front could have been totally empty, and the back full of blacks, but I still went to the back. It was expected.

Blacks treated each other badly, too. The law just didn't hold up for black-on-black crimes. A black person could kill or harm another black person be arrested, only to be out of jail and back to plowing their white employers' fields the next day. Nothing would happen to the assailant or murderer. To the law back then, it was just one less *nigger* to worry about. But if you hurt or killed a white person, it meant a lynching or beating or a long prison sentence.

That's the environment in which I grew up. There was a lot of persecution and hatred coming from white folks, but then there were these pockets of love, too. People like Mrs. McCrary and Mr. Burks kept me from hating white people in return. I had my moments just like anybody else, but Mama taught me to see the individual, not the entire race—and to trust that God could change the hearts of even the most wretched among us.

Later, when I was much older, I would study the men and women I admired, like Rosa Parks, Dr. Martin Luther King Jr., and Mahatma Gandhi, among others—men and women who embodied godly grace, who advocated love and peaceful resistance to persecution rather than hatred and violent retaliation. One quote from Gandhi sums up the human struggle to relate to one another: *"I know, to banish anger altogether from one's breast is a difficult task. It cannot be achieved through pure personal effort. It can be done only by God's grace."*

That is so true! We are powerless on our own because our natural man or woman is plagued by a sinful inclination. Thus, we must lift ourselves to cry into the breast of God. There, He hears us, wipes our tears, and grants us an allotment of grace to bestow upon our merciless brethren. *"Fear not, for I am with you; be not dismayed, for I am your God. I will strengthen you, yes I will help you, I will uphold you with my righteous right hand,"* Isaiah 41:10 (NKJV)

Even at 16 years old and after we had moved onto our own farm, Mr. And Mrs. McCrary still came to visit and still gave me birthday gifts every year. Much later, after I returned from the Army on furlough, Mama insisted on taking me to visit the McCrary's and Mr. Burks, both of whom wanted to see me whenever I came home. I still had to go to their back doors. There were appearances to consider, after all. After having served in the military during the Korean War, the thought of having to go to the back door of anybody's house just ate me up inside. I abided to make Mama comfortable.

Things were a little different after we moved to the Rivers Burks Plantation because we were no longer living in a town. The Rivers Burks sat outside of Byhalia by several miles, which limited interaction with white folks. There was only a corner store owned by a white guy named Mr. Clark. He turned out to be a pretty nice man, too. Mama would send us over there with a note to buy some bologna and wieners to eat while we worked the fields. I'd walk in, and Mr. Clark would say, "All right, boy, where's that note your mama gave you?"

I'd hand it to him, and he'd fill the order. Once he was finished, he'd write down what we had gotten, and Mama would come in whenever she got the money to pay the bill. She never missed paying. In fact, I just used this story recently in a sermon I was preaching on the value of relationships. That relationship between my Mama and Mr. Clark allowed us to get the food we needed, even though we wouldn't be able to pay until later.

We didn't have to live in fear because we did what was expected of us. But get out of line with the white folks at that time in our history, and you could get yourself hung! I never saw it happen, but I heard about it happening. A black man named Walter had gotten into a fight with a white guy in town. Well, a bunch of whites jumped him afterward and told Walter he had better apologize or pay a heavy price. Walter chose to spit on those white men instead. They hooked him to the bumper of a truck dragged him through the streets until he was dead. Not a thing happened to those white men, either! That's just the way it was in those days for southern blacks. But the white lawmen and townsfolk made sure all the blacks in Byhalia knew what had happened to Walter, lest anybody else try the same thing.

Discrimination, bigotry, racism, and mistreatment were prevalent. We'd go to the local movie house where Negroes had to sit upstairs in the smaller balcony, the whites would sit down below. Some dummy threw a crumpled piece of paper that landed down below on some white folks. The manager stormed upstairs and said, "All right! Who did that?"

Nobody said a word.

The manager went up to one boy, grabbed him by the collar, and shook him violently. "You know who did it! Speak up!"

The boy cowered and said, "No, sir. I didn't see nothing."

The manager said, "You're lying, boy. All you niggers get out of here! Right now!"

We had all paid our little 25 cents, but we had to leave and without a refund. Must have been 60 of us, and the manager kept every bit of our money!

Ugly incidents like those were fairly common in Mississippi, stirring up a lot of hatred in the hearts of black folks. I wasn't immune to hatred either, but every time an evil thought would enter my mind about white injustice, Mrs. McCrary and her love for my mother and me would enter my mind. People like Mr. Rivers Burks would come to mind too—how he went and got a truck, took us in, taught me how to operate equipment, many adults didn't even know how to operate, how he let me work sometimes in his sawmill and how he gave me a little pocket money every Saturday when my father was away in the Army. And Mr. Clark from the corner store, how he extended his line of credit to my mother—a Mississippi black woman.

Those things aside, I have seen some amazing changes in my lifetime! Not only has technology changed dramatically, but so have relationships between people of different colors. I have seen forced segregation and forced integration. I have experienced hatred, and I have experienced love. But perhaps nothing has been more dramatic for me than living long enough to see the first black president elected to office in the United States. As a Republican, I may disagree with the man on certain things, but that the man was elected at all tells me something about this country that I love— that we are no longer limited by color or pedigree nor bound by party or poverty. We have attained the unattainable, and I am grateful to our Lord for that.

## MY TWO GREAT GRANDFATHERS—FORMER SLAVES

Great Grandpa Andrew Caruthers was about 112 years old when he died in February 1948. About a year prior, when he was 111 years old, we kids would still bring him a cord of wood, and he would work all day chopping that wood into finer pieces. How remarkably fit he was for a man over a century old! He'd have a whole cord of wood cut up for the fire. That's a lot of wood to cut for any man. And he still had most of his teeth at 112. Great Grandpa Caruthers, on the other hand, had a big knot on his head from a beating he had taken during his slave days. He'd rub that knot all the time. Sometimes, he'd say to me, "Son, come here and rub Grandpa's head for him."

I'd say, "Grandpa, you rub it."

Then he'd say affectionately, "But it feels so much better when you rub it, Henry."

He'd tell us ghost stories that would keep us up at night, too. After hearing his frightful tellings, we'd be too afraid to sleep. After though, he would say, "Ah no, Grandpa was just playing. You just remember that God takes care of you no matter who shows up."

He always spoke about the goodness of God.

He lived with us when we were sharecropping on the McAuley and the Rivers Burks plantations. He did not, however, live with us on the McCrary Plantation, something that didn't make much sense until I started writing this book. He is in the photo below, standing on the left, his silvery mustache shining in the Mississippi sun.

In the process of searching the Internet for an old photo of Ada Dee McCrary, I happened upon a photo of the gravestone for Ada Dee and her husband, Ingram. If you look at the names on the combined marker (they were buried together), you can see Ada Dee's maiden name listed as Caruthers, the same surname as my Great-Grandfather Caruthers. If his owners had given him their surname while he was a slave, then it's likely that somewhere down the line, Ada Dee's family owned my family on my mother's side. That, to me, was an amazing discovery! It also explained why my Great-Great Grandpa Caruthers didn't want to live on the McCrary plantation with us.

Perhaps seeing Ada Dee every day would have hit too close to his heart. It also leads me to wonder if we are somehow *related* to Ada Dee *Caruthers* McCrary? Is that why she'd been so loving toward us? I wish I knew the answer to that question. Maybe one day, God will shed light on that mystery.

Great-Great Grandpa Caruthers had no education but was highly intelligent and brilliant, in my opinion. We had no television back then. He would sit on the shady side of the house when we left on Sunday for church. When we got home, my Grandpa Caruthers would ask us what passage the preacher had spoken on that day. We could tell him just the verse number and book, and he would quote the verse. The man knew his Bible! He'd bow his silvery head, and his eyes would get teary as he contemplated what the preacher taught. He was a thin man but solid, about 6', with a big white mustache. I can see his face as if he were standing here before me today. God knows I loved him! He was just a special man in my life!

Great-Great-Grandpa Caruthers would sit around and tell us about his slave days, about how some of the other blacks would tell fibs when they were caught doing something bad, saying it was him so he'd get whipped for their transgressions. He kept his mouth quiet—not unlike Jesus—took his licks and trusted God for the rest. I'm not sure where he learned about Jesus, maybe from his white slave owners who considered themselves Christians. Maybe he memorized scripture while sitting in church service. If I remember correctly, he didn't know how to read. In any event, Great-Grandpa Caruthers became a wonderful man of God despite the persecution and his lack of education.

You know, I've been asked by a lot of people over the years why I don't hate white people for the things I've seen and experienced. There are many good reasons not to hate, and that goes for hating anybody. I suppose one of the things keeping me from being bitter toward white people is that I honestly believe the whites back then, particularly during the slave days, saw us not as human beings but as property, part of their living. We weren't livestock in the traditional sense, but we were likely seen as just another animal to be sold or used for profit. I'm not sure it was entirely malicious. Some likely acted out of ignorance, like the herd following the lead cow over a cliff.

Thank God those times have changed! Besides, if I'm being honest, blacks weren't entirely blameless in the slave trade. Early on, it was our own people in Africa who would trap future slaves. The slave ship captain would tell the African hunters what type of black Africans they wanted, and the hunters would then trap us and sell us to the whites. Then the white crew would sail the slave ship back to America, or Brazil (who, by the way, was the worst perpetrator of slavery), Britain, or France, or wherever there might be a market, and sell us to slave owners. That's just the way it was, like it or not. Alex Haley, whom I met some years ago, chronicled this process in his wonderful book on slavery, *Roots*. It isn't an easy pill for blacks to swallow, but it's one we must acknowledge and accept if we want healing.

Like I've already mentioned, some whites knew better and treated us like fellow human beings. That's how my family on my father's side got those 300 acres. A white family gave it to my great-granddaddy, Lump Hearn, because they felt badly about the way they had treated him. They wanted to make amends. When they freed my great-grandfather, "the brothers," as he sometimes called them, set him up so he could be a success. He called them "the brothers" because, way back, the white owners had sexual relations with some of their slaves. Great-Granddaddy Lump was related to them, though that much was kept secret while still in the brothers' care. I suppose that's one of the reasons I look as light-skinned as I do and why my grandfather Percy Hearn looked practically white. As the brothers developed, they came to care about their black brother and wanted to do right, so they gave him the 300 acres. This was a gift from the plantation owners, not the government. They were not abolitionists, but two of the brothers who had grown up in the Mississippi area saw the wrong in what was happening and gave Great-Granddaddy Lump the property. I get emotional just thinking about that good fortune!

Great-Granddaddy Hearn and Great-Grandpa Caruthers hadn't met until after Caruthers moved in with us. Hearn was living on his 300 acres and was what other Negroes called a "big shot nigger," because he owned land and had lighter skin. My cousin Zell on the Hearn side of our family attended school with me for a while. She sported mink-type coats and new clothes while the rest of us wore hand-me-down white kids' clothing or handmade shirts and pants. She wasn't allowed to sit with us either. Even our black teachers recognized the difference between Zell and the rest of us.

By now you might be wondering why we weren't living on that 300 acres as well. The way I understand it, my father left home when he was only 12 years old. Great-Granddaddy Lump's farm was on the north side of Highway 78, which split Byhalia. Our school was just to the south, a couple miles away. Lump and his wife had 14 kids in all, including Percy, my father's father. Daddy couldn't get along with Percy or Lump, so he moved in above the garage of Dr. McAuley's house. The doctor offered my father a driving job and he took it. Daddy never went back home. He couldn't get along with them and wanted a different life for himself, though at that time, he didn't know exactly what that meant. He drove for the doctor for at least 10 years until Dr. McAuley had Daddy drafted into the Army.

My father and the Hearn side of the family mended fences after Daddy gave his life to Christ. I would say to my father, "It's not really right to be hating your family."

He would say, "I know what I'm doing, boy."

God worked it out in His time. In regard to the land, Daddy had his own 60-acre farm by the time Lump died, so he made no fuss about getting a piece of the 300 acres.

In writing this chapter, I'm reminded of a sad truth still relevant today: Prejudice is a human condition exclusive to no gender, no race, no age group, no political party and no religion. It is a form of bondage that plagues us all, and the only way to set ourselves free is through *grace*. Prejudice answered with prejudice only begets more prejudice. But prejudice answered with grace breaks the cycle and ends the heartache. Grace always heals.

CHAPTER SIX

# THE GOOD AND GRACIOUS SAMARITAN

After my father left for the Army during WWII (though he only went as far as Fort Jackson, South Carolina), Dr. McAuley told us to get out; the same man who had my father drafted, perhaps Dr. McAuley thought my father was getting a little too ambitious in his thinking, wanting to own a farm eventually. Perhaps he and my father had an argument, though that would have resulted in more than a draft notice back then, more like a beating or lynching. There is no way of knowing for sure the motivation behind Dr. McAuley's actions regarding my father, who had driven for Dr. McAuley since he was 12 years old. Whatever the cause, the doctor intended to harm our family. That much was obvious. But what Dr. McAuley intended for bad, God used for good.

We met Mr. Rivers Burks. Mr. Burks turned out to be a saint. Oh, he still kept up appearances with other white folks for the sake of business, but even then, he was always respectful toward us. Behind the scenes, out of sight of condemning eyes, Mr. Burks blessed us tremendously! I sure hope he went to be with Jesus when he left this world because he was such a good man. I managed to find this old photo of Mr. Burks taken at his store in 1929 before I was born. In the background, you can see the

"White" only restrooms, designated by the sign above the entry. On the opposite side would have been the "Colored" only restrooms.

Even though this photo was taken before I was born, the store layout remained the same. The entry to his café would have been directly across from where he is standing, if I remember correctly.

The Rivers Burks Plantation took up a big chunk of Miller, Mississippi, a town about five miles northwest outside of Byhalia. Rivers Burks started in Miller and continued all the way up around to Miller-Center Hill. It was about 900 acres of mostly all cotton, and he also raised soybeans. Mr. Burks, having all that land to farm, needed somebody that could operate the various pieces of farm equipment. I didn't know the first thing about the modern machinery Mr. Burks owned, but I guess he must have seen my eyes light up whenever I got around a piece. One day he said, "Henry, I need somebody that can operate this here equipment, and I was thinking you just might be the one for the job. How would you feel about that? I'll work you hard, but I'll teach you how to operate all this equipment."

Well, I'd have jumped out of my shoes if I'd been wearing any. "Yes, sir!" I proclaimed, beaming like the stars. "I'm a hard worker. If you'll teach me, Mr. Rivers (that's how I referred to him), I know I can do a good job."

Mr. Burks taught me how to operate the tillers, combines, balers, trucks, plows and so much more. For a young kid with a mechanical curiosity, it was like being in heaven! I loved, loved, loved operating those machines! And sometimes, I would catch a glimpse of Mama standing there, looking at me doing a skilled man's work, and I could see how proud she was of her boy.

Mr. Burks did something else for us that just wasn't done back then. He went to Citizens Bank in Byhalia and opened a bank account for Mama and me. Blacks in 1930s and 40s Mississippi weren't allowed to have bank accounts. He cared so much for our family that he opened accounts for us.

Somehow, the government subsidized our living while Daddy was away in the Army, mailing a monthly stipend to us to make up for the loss of income my father would have provided. I'm not sure how much we received every month, but I know it wasn't much. Still, Mr. Burks told Mama, "You take everything the government sends you because your husband is away in the Army, and you put that into your account and save it, Bertha. Whatever money you need to buy food and clothing for your kids, borrow that from me against the cotton you pick. Then your money is locked in, and when your husband gets home, you'll be able to buy your own farm." Wow!

Mama used to carry a white handkerchief with her because she would get to crying when something good happened, praising Jesus for the blessing. She said to him, "Mr. Burks, why would you do that for us?"

He answered, "Well, Bertha, that's just what I'm supposed to do. It doesn't cost me anything, and when Red gets home, you'll have the money to buy your property. I suggest you not even tell Red you've got the money because when they put them in the Army, they feed them funny stuff that gets them thinking strange things. You don't want to lose your money because of that. Save it until you have enough to purchase the farm, and then tell him. You will not need to rely on me or anybody else any longer."

That act of kindness by Mr. Burks changed our lives forever. But a funny incident would happen before we bore the fruit of his grace.

Daddy had been gone for about two years by the time he returned from the Army and Fort Jackson. I had learned how to operate all the farm equipment, though I was only about 10 years old and was hard at work when Daddy arrived home. It must have been about 10 a.m. or so, and I was way off on the property. I could see Daddy walking across the rolling landscape. I knew him by his walk—and something was wrong. He approached with a clenched jaw and determined steps.

When he reached me, Daddy said, "Shut it down, boy!" I did, and he asked, "Henry, who told you to operate this tractor?"

"Mr. Rivers," I said reluctantly.

"Get down off that machine. Leave it right there."

He grabbed me by the hand, leading me as he stormed back across the field, back to the tool shed where Mr. Burks was working. When he got to the tool shed, Daddy said, "Mr. Burks, when did you ever have any black kids? You don't tell my boy—"

"Now hold up, Red," Mr. Burks interrupted.

Daddy said, "You don't tell me to hold up! That's my boy, and when you want my boy to do something, you ask me!"

Mr. Burks said, "Red, you weren't here."

Daddy picked up a heavy singletree, a bar mechanism made of wood and steel that was used to hook a mule to the plow, and started to raise it over his head like he was going to beat Mr. Burks with it.

Mr. Burks jumped into his truck and raced over to our house to talk to Mama. She later told me Mr. Burks rushed in, saying, "I told you the

Army feeds them stuff that makes them crazy! Red is after me. He wants to kill me!"

That was back in 1943, so all Mr. Burks had to do was turn my father in, and the law would have hung him, no questions asked. But instead, Mr. Burks went to my mother and said, "Now, Red's going to be coming over that hill in a minute chasing me. Make him behave, Bertha. Don't let him bother me because I don't want anything to do with that."

When Daddy and I got there, Mama intercepted Daddy, pushing him back while saying, "Red! Red!"

Daddy yelled, "You get out of the way!"

But Mama managed to calm him down by saying, "Red, you can't be doing that. They've killed men for less."

Daddy quieted down, took a few minutes to settle, and then apologized. "I'm so sorry, Mr. Burks."

Mr. Burks said, "Red, it's all right. I know you've been through some stuff. It's all right."

Daddy said, "I know you could have me arrested and put in jail for life for what I tried to do. I'm so sorry."

Mr. Burks said, "We aren't into that. You're a part of this farm. I care about you."

It wasn't long after that incident that Mr. Rivers found the 60-acre farm for us. A guy named Charley Harriway carried the deed. Charlie was black and owned a big piece of property he'd broken up into 60-acre parcels to sell. Each parcel had a price of $2,000. Mr. Burks went back and talked to Mama about it, telling her, "Now might be a good time to tell Red about the money you've saved, Bertha."

Mama had saved about $5,000 total—enough to buy the land and build a small house on it. When they told him about the money, my father looked confused for a moment, tilting his head as if trying to figure it out. After he reconciled the reality in his mind, Daddy turned to Mr. Burks and said, "You did that for us?"

Mr. Burks said with a big grin, "Yes. Did I do all right?" "Yes, but a while ago, I was ready to kill you."

"Yes, but you didn't know what you were doing," Mr. Burks said. "You guys have been the best workers on my farm, and you deserve to have your own place. Now, when you all want to see it, you can borrow my truck and go take a look."

My beloved parents ended up buying the place. Daddy hired a contractor and architect named Elick Nelson to build it. Our new home had an inside bathroom—first time ever for us! We had electricity and indoor plumbing as well — two other firsts. I'm getting emotional just thinking about it! I have a picture of the house below.

It was an exciting time for our family. We had always lived in drafty, old homes. Now, we had a house that sealed up tight against the weather. We had our own farm and our own home with indoor everything. We had found our own little Promised Land!

God richly blesses His faithful! Dr. McAuley had intended to hurt our family by having my father drafted into the Army, but God used it for good, bringing a Good Samaritan, Mr. Burks, into our lives to help my mother save all the money the Army paid us while my father was indentured. Had my father not been drafted, the Army would not have paid that money to us, and we would not have been able to purchase the farm nor build the house. By having Mr. Burks teach me how to operate all the modern farm equipment, God had prepared us for owning our own plantation. It just goes to show that *"all things work for the good of those who believe and who wait patiently, trusting in the Lord for His provision."* (Romans 8:28 NKJ)

CHAPTER SEVEN

# DEACON FETTERSON AND HOW I CAME TO "FESS-A-LIGION"

I was 12 years old when I willingly and formally gave my life to the Lord. We were having revivals at the time—so many revivals that sometimes we'd have them twice a day, one around 10 a.m., another in the evening, maybe about 7. Sometimes, a traveling preacher would lead the revival; sometimes, a local reverend would. When I came to "fess-a-ligion," as we called it, I did it during one of those revivals with Reverend Hibler, our regular pastor.

"Fessin-a-ligion" (short for confessing your religion) was a moment of transformation, a time when you would feel the Holy Spirit take hold of your life, causing you to jump up off the "mourner's bench" and start thanking the Lord out loud.

Now, the "mourners bench" was a long bench where those kids who had not "fessed-a-ligion" would sit. The older folks would come by and pray over them, hoping the Holy Spirit would lead them to confess their faith soon. Our congregation sang this song, low and slow: *"Oh, come on you mourners . . . into the arrrrmy! Oh, come oh you mourners into the arrrrmy!"*

What the singers meant was that they were part of the army of God, but we who hadn't "fessed-a-ligion" weren't. They were calling us to join them.

Well, one week, we had a five-day, mid-week revival held in the evenings so most everybody could attend. These were lively affairs and a lot of fun for those not on the mourner's bench. It wasn't that we were being shamed on the bench, but somehow, it seemed a lower place to be. Every night, the preacher would proclaim the loving grace of our Lord, then offer those on the bench the chance to confess their faith. I'd been on the mourner's bench all the way up to Friday night. Nothing happened to me on Monday. Nothing Tuesday. Wednesday passed uneventfully. Thursday came and went, too. So, on Friday evening, about an hour before the revival was scheduled to begin, Deacon Fetterson, with whom I had a special relationship, came out to the ball field to pay me a special visit. We kids played ball north of the church before most services, and I was the catcher. Deacon Fetterson pulled me aside and said, "Son, now, you got to fess-a-ligion. Don't be wasting this opportunity. God is calling you, Son."

So that Friday night, after the preacher had brought God's word, I leaped off the bench and "fessed-a-legion," shouting things like, "Praise Him! Praise His holy name!" Even though I still had doubts in my mind, I didn't tell anybody about those doubts, but I had them nonetheless. I had doubts about this Jesus whom I couldn't see. But that night, I came off the bench and confessed my faith in Christ, making Deacon Fetterson so happy. Mama, she lit up like a candle! She ran and shouted and gave God praise when she found out her oldest son had given his life to Christ. I didn't have the heart to tell her that I only declared my faith to get off of that bench. The only time I saw my mother happier was when my father gave *his* life to the Lord a little later and at a different church. I got saved at the New Zion Baptist Church. He got saved at the Nickel Chapel Methodist Church.

After that, the elders really thought I was something special. I taught Sunday School for two years before they made me a deacon. Then, the elders ordained me like they did the men and put me over the Sunday school. Deacon Fetterson said to me one day, "Son, you don't know where you're gonna be. Deacon Fetterson might be gone by then, but you gonna be a great man! You got something that the Lord done set up for you, Son, so you got to start living different than the others. Now, I know your daddy done had this talk with you, but with the girls, you gotta keep your britches on, Son. You gotta keep those britches on!"

That causes me to laugh now, but when he said those words, "You gotta keep those britches on!" I took them to heart. I wasn't that interested in girls anyway because of what had happened to me when I was 8 years old in that pasture.

"He done set up something for you," Deacon Fetterson reiterated. He meant God had a calling for me, which, of course, turned out to be prophetic. I had never really thought about becoming a pastor, though, not until I was 20 or 21 years old. Those thoughts hadn't entered my mind until I went off to Korea.

That experience of "fessin-a-ligion" reminds me that we have to simply take it on faith that God exists and that He alone has the power to change our lives. Once we accept that as fact, we then need to get out of the way and let God work in us.

CHAPTER EIGHT

# OUR OWN LITTLE PROMISED LAND

Time, it would seem, is the Lord's currency. He doles out more to some less to others, but all of His children receive a measure. My parents, especially Mama, knew this better than most, always waiting in faithful trust for the Lord's provision, particularly when it came to purchasing their own farm.

Very few blacks were landowners back in the 1930s and 40s. Many people today cite the *40 Acres and a Mule* policy implemented shortly after the American Civil War by General William Tecumseh Sherman as a denial of this fact, but the truth is that this "policy" was actually a *Special Field Order* only, issued by General Sherman in 1865 after his "March to the Sea"—an order President Abraham Lincoln let stand.

The idea behind the *40 Acres and a Mule* order was to provide slaves freed from confederates (freedmen) with a means to be free and self-supportive. At one point, it was estimated that about 10,000 freed slaves occupied approximately 400,000 acres of Georgia and South Carolina. What a lot of people fail to realize, however, is that Lincoln's successor, President Andrew Johnson, a Democrat from Tennessee, revoked General Sherman's order, returning the 400,000 acres to their original white landowners. President Andrew Johnson, the first American president ever to face impeachment, also opposed the Fourteenth Amendment to the Constitution, which finally granted American citizenship to male blacks. I mention that not to continue beating the drum of racism but rather to emphasize that though the Thirteenth Amendment of the Constitution put an end to slavery in the United States, and the Fourteenth Amendment finally granted blacks in America citizenship (males only), discrepancies between opportunities afforded blacks and whites were still enormous. It remained so until the Civil Rights Movements of the 1950s, 60s, and 70s forced a much-needed correction. That my parents were able to buy their own 60-acre farm in the 1940s was a testament to the power of *persistence*, to the power of *loving grace* shown a black family by a white land and business owner, Mr. Rivers Burks, and to the power of God's *mercy*, which is always right on time. It reminds me of a verse I've preached on many times: *"But those who wait on the LORD shall renew their strength; they shall mount up with wings like eagles; they shall run and not be weary; they shall walk and not faint."*—Isaiah 40:30-33 (NKJV)

Our 60-acre farm was located in the rolling countryside of Center Hill, Mississippi, just a few miles on one side from the Tennessee border and just a few miles from Mr. Rivers Burks' place on the other side. I remember when we viewed that piece of land for the very first time as a family. To my parents, that parcel was the Promised Land! They envisioned it soon flowing with undulating rows of pillowy cotton, though not the Bible's milk and honey. That moment will forever be embedded in my memory. The sense of pride my parents felt as they gazed upon the green fields that were now theirs by a deed of ownership. There were tears and they hugged us children. They had achieved what few blacks at that time had done—they'd become landowners. But the owning of land had much more significance to them than just achievement. To my parents, it meant true freedom—the freedom to follow God's lead and not man's, the freedom to live as they chose, without having to ask permission. On that 60-acre plot of American soil, my folks were able to walk where they wanted, plant what they wanted, eat when they wanted, worship when they wanted, and rest when they wanted. They were not subject to another's leave on that 60--acres, and that was worth more to them than gold.

Once the deed transferred and my parents took ownership, Daddy got to designing and building the house with an architect while Mama and us kids got to tilling and planting. We suddenly had a lot of responsibility on our hands. If we didn't sow, we wouldn't reap. That was and continues to be the responsibility of true freedom. Daddy still worked at the airlines, though, until the house was finished and we had a crop to sell. Mama still worked for Mr. Dale Armor, the man who purchased Mr. Burks' plantation not too long after we bought our farm, though that work for Mr. Armor would taper off as the crop grew and our house neared completion. Mr. Armor was a kind man and allowed us to keep living on his plantation until we had a house to live in of our own.

The house turned out to be beautiful! Daddy had it built, like so many homes in the South, on the crest of a rolling hill and with an elevated foundation, which helped counter flooding caused by frequent Mississippi rainstorms. We had a modest front porch from which to enjoy lemonade and leisurely fellowship as a family. We were witness to many colorful evening sunsets from that porch. The dusky Mississippi sky turned fire-red as it touched the western horizon, blending to purple then black as it melted away back toward the east, stars just starting to twinkle. There were three bedrooms: one for the boys, one for the girls, and one for my parents. Best of all, we had electricity, a window-mounted air conditioner, indoor plumbing, and an indoor bathroom! You really come to appreciate an indoor toilet when hurricane-force winds and heavy rains are raging outside! Praise the Lord for His grace!

The moist northern Mississippi soil on which our acreage sat teamed with nutrients. So many crops could have been grown there, but my parents settled on cotton as the cash crop. We would plant other things, like vegetables and a few fruit trees, but cotton was the crop my parents knew best. And we had some livestock—horses and mules that we used for plowing and tilling the land, cows for beef and milk, hogs for pork, and chickens for eggs. Later on, Daddy built his own little lake on the property, which he stocked with his favorite species of fish. Mostly, though, the small lake helped water our livestock, as well as provide an isolated oasis for ducks and swans. The property also had an overabundance of trees that we would sometimes cut and sell to the timber companies. The only motor-driven piece of machinery was Daddy's Chevrolet truck, which he bought new shortly after we moved onto the farm.

I lived on that 60-acre farm for three more years before getting drafted into the military. But my parents lived there for the rest of their lives, making good money by raising and selling cotton. They'd get about $500 for a bale of cotton, and in those days, that was a lot of money! Shoot! I mean a lot of money! We'd get the same price as the white farmers. Daddy was a sharp businessman. We didn't own a cotton gin. We'd pick our crop and take it to the local ginner. They would also buy the seeds from us, but they'd take some of the seeds as payment for ginning the cotton. It was a barter system that seemed to satisfy all involved.

Buyers would come by and look at the "pull"—the length of pull of our particular brand of cotton grown. Our brand had a long pull, so we got premium price. At the end of the year, we would pull the scrap cotton, which had less pull. We got less money for that crop, though. The particular species of cotton we raised was DP&L (Delta Pine and Land Company) #14, I believe, which required 1,400 pounds of cotton with seeds in it to make a 500-bale of seedless cotton. Once we got to 1,400 pounds of cotton, we'd go to the gin.

Picking cotton was hard on the hands, but our hands toughened up with time. We learned how to fit our fingers into the plant to get at the cotton without too much pain. We'd then put it into our carrying bag, which would hold as much as 60 pounds.

My daughter and I drove up to Coalinga, California, not too long ago and went past rows and rows of cotton that pickers bundled and stacked beside the highway. I wanted to stop so badly! Seeing those bales of cotton took me back home to the Mississippi of my youth. Despite the racial tension and oppression happening around us at the time, we managed to enjoy working together as a family. We'd sing hymns and songs while we picked, mainly to get our minds off of hardships and to remind us of God's blessings. Mama just loved the Lord, and she wasted no minute expressing it to Him!

Mama believed in taking every opportunity to glorify God with her lips, singing and rejoicing and praying without ceasing, as the Apostle Paul tells us in 1 Thessalonians 5:16-18 (KJV) *"Rejoice always, pray without ceasing. In everything give thanks; for this is the will of God in Christ Jesus concerning you."* Inadvertently, Mother glorified Him by her example. I like to call it "being continually in His presence." I, too, take every opportunity to be in the presence of my Lord. If I seem happy, if I am able to love all people, as I hope to do always, it is because God is continually with me.

We children decided to sell the family farm after mother and father went on to heaven. That decision broke my heart. My sisters and brothers built lives for themselves elsewhere and could not move back to the farm. I would have gladly bought them out, but I could not afford it. Had I the money, I would have kept my parents' farm, possibly even resuming my life as a cotton farmer. God had other plans for me, I suppose. Now, it's developed with residential units, but there is a tribute to our family right in the middle of the development—a street named *Hearns Cove*. That really was a nice gesture, and it meant a lot to us kids. One day, I'd like to go back there and buy one of those units on Hearns Cove, just to keep a little something in the family.

In reading back over my words in this chapter, I'm reminded of a very important lesson that all should learn: By remaining in the continual presence of God and His endless grace, we are able to remain free of the world's trappings, including retaliating for wrongs suffered and responding to hateful vitriol. If we are not walking continually with Christ, we will have moments where we walk with the world, and it is there that we find anxiety, discord, and heartache.

CHAPTER NINE

# THE HEART KNOWS—ESSIE (AN INTRODUCTION)

M eeting my wife for the first time was an enchanted moment, the kind that only happens in fairytales and movies, not in real life.

It was late 1948 because the autumn leaves had already fallen, along with the southern temperatures. The green rolling hillsides had turned an undulating gold, the wild grass swaying and dancing with the breeze, its enthusiasm contained only by railed wooden fence lines. Between the endless fence lines were dirt roads, each leading somewhere or another, one of which I was traveling, leading our mule-driven wagon, which was loaded to overflowing with our family's belongings. Two of my

sisters rode on the bench, laughing about something. They were always laughing about something.

At some point, I began to get thirsty. It was common in those days for people traveling in rural areas of the South to search out a home to ask for water or food. Stores were scarce, and at that time in our history, bottled water wasn't even a thought. If you carried water with you, it was in a canteen or barrel, neither of which we had brought on that trip. We were nearing our farm, but I just couldn't wait. I needed a drink and went up to the house situated on the farm next to ours. I knocked, hurrying to dust off my trousers and straighten my clothes before somebody answered, and when the heavy, wooden door swung open, there she was, beautiful like a night sky full of stars! She had on a white headscarf, which I supposed kept the hair out of her face while she worked, and her long, plaid, cotton floor-length dress modestly draped her figure. Her skin was dark bronze, her inviting eyes were translucent brown, and her smile was warm but suspiciously shy.

"Yes?" she said, sweet like the song of a white-crowned sparrow, happy that the sun has just risen. "Can I help you?"

Well, I just about fell off the porch, unable to speak for a moment, suddenly embarrassed at the way I looked, my denim overalls patched in places, and my skin dusty from traveling miles of dirt roads with the mules and wagon.

"Yes?" she said again.

That's when her father swung the door wider and came alongside of her, his arm draped over her shoulder.

"What is it, son?" he asked.

"I'm thirsty, sir," was about all I could manage, my eyes still transfixed on his daughter.

"Get this young man a tall glass of water, Essie," he commanded in a loving but deep voice.

*The Heart Knows—Essie (An Introduction)*

*Essie.* It was the first time I had heard her name, and it resonated through my bones, all the way down to my toes and back again. *Essie.* Well, I must have looked dazed or something because right then, he asked me, "Are you all right, boy? You ill or something?"

Essie saved me from answering by returning with the glass of cool water. She reached out to hand it to me, but I guess I just let it hang while I stared at her face.

"Son, now you're scaring me, boy. If you're thirsty, drink. If not—"

Right then, I grabbed the glass, downed it in just a couple gulps, and then bolted from their porch, tripping over myself along the way. When I got back to the wagon, my sisters were wondering if I had bothered to get them any water. They had been watching the whole affair and began to laugh at me as I led the mule wagon away.

"She sure was purdy!" I mumbled, loud enough for my sisters to hear, though.

"Too pretty for you!" one of them said.

"I'm gonna marry that girl. One day, I'm gonna marry that Essie." Well, that just killed them. They fell about themselves in laughter, telling me to concentrate on pulling the wagon like a good little boy. Essie, I kept thinking. Essie.

Another wonderful thing about Essie was that she lived on the farm adjoining ours. That meant I would have occasion to see her and get to know her. I was also pleasantly surprised that when I showed up for my first day at my new schoolhouse, Essie was there. It was a stroke of divine providence!

Her full name was Essie May Brocks, and she was 14 years old, just two years younger than me. She was ahead of me in schooling. I would need to move quickly if I wanted to capitalize on that opportunity. That was her last year there, and it was already halfway over. Once she graduated the eighth grade at New Halliburton School, Essie went on to Collierville

Junior High School in Tennessee, which allowed black students to attend until the tenth grade, unlike Mississippi, which only allowed blacks up to an eighth-grade education. Our farms were only a few miles from the Tennessee border, and Collierville Junior High School was just on the other side.

Once Essie moved on to Collierville, I determined that I would go there as well. As soon as I was able, I transferred, with the help of Mr. Poole, my New Halliburton teacher, and with the guidance of Mr. Otis L. Armor, who was principal at Collierville Junior High School. The only way we Mississippi black children could attend a Tennessee school was with a Tennessee address. Mr. Armor and Mr. Poole worked numerous sources to make that happen. They were active in getting blacks from Mississippi educated, even though they risked their own careers in the process. I cannot speak to whether God would condone or condemn such craftiness, but I do know God would condemn the prejudicial practices of the Mississippi government in regard to the education of blacks. The only choices for black students wanting schooling past the eighth grade in Mississippi were, in essence, to break the law or to accept the limitations imposed upon us by the Mississippi Legislature. Neither choice was a good one. Some families actually relocated to Tennessee, but my family had just purchased a farm. We weren't going anywhere.

Still, Essie was heading off to attend school at Collierville Junior High School, and if that's where Essie was going, I wanted to go too, even if it meant crossing the Tennessee border every day to make it happen. I just knew she would be my wife one day, so much so that I told her as much.

She responded, "I already have a boyfriend, Henry. I'm sorry." I said, "That's okay. I'll wait on you to break that up."

While at Collierville, we would find time to spend together, often getting ice cream or treats from the snack bar at school. She'd come watch me play baseball with the boys, too. When she didn't want to, I would tell

## The Heart Knows—Essie (An Introduction)

her I needed her there to hold my money and things while I played. The following are our class photos from Collierville, taken in 1952, according to the print at the bottom:

Essie was the first girl I showed interest in after the molestation I'd experienced at 8 years old. There were other girls I thought were pretty, but my heart belonged to Essie, even if hers didn't belong to me. Things continued that way until I turned 19 and left for the Army. Essie's mother had died due to a breech birth when Essie was only 3 years old, leaving her father, Sylvester Brooks, to raise her alone. They loved each other greatly. Somehow, though, I think that experience of being raised without a mother affected her. How it related to me exactly was unclear, but I couldn't shake the feeling that it did contribute to her reluctance in dating me. Her father, on the other hand, thought the sun rose and set with me and wanted desperately for Essie and me to marry. But Essie wouldn't even commit to being engaged. Perhaps I wasn't Essie's type of guy. The boy she liked, Charlie Taylor, drove a beautiful, brand new, sparkling black Buick. I didn't have anything but a mule and wagon. His father owned a mortuary and had built a small fortune for his family.

My parents were just starting out in business and hadn't accumulated anything yet.

In truth, Essie's denial of me broke my heart. But what could I do? The draft was on for the Korean War and the Army had come calling. My pursuit of Essie would have to wait until after I returned if I returned. Then something remarkable happened. Essie's father discovered that Charlie Taylor and Essie were somehow related, meaning they could not marry. The kinship alluded to by Essie's father is still unclear to this day, making me believe that it may have been a ploy to keep Essie from marrying him. In either event, it worked. Essie broke it off with Charlie and committed to waiting for me to return from Korea before deciding on whom to marry. But I wanted to marry her before I left, and my youthful impatience would lead me to go Absent Without Leave (AWOL) from the Army, something for which the military had no tolerance.

I'll get into that more in the next chapter, but for now, I think it's important to note that sometimes bitterness is the easier choice in a moment of rejection, but not the best choice. Time, persistence, and patience are the better choices overall. These three allow both people to find the grace to love one another. If grace does show itself, then perhaps the relationship is God's will after all. If grace does not show itself, then acceptance of the outcome is the only choice, as any relationship void of grace is doomed to fail.

CHAPTER TEN

# ONWARD CHRISTIAN SOLDIER—THE ARMY CALLS

When the Draft Board sent me a letter in 1952, my father, with the help of someone else—perhaps Mr. Burks—was able to get my enlistment delayed for one year. The military granted temporary waivers for the sons of farmers, sons who were essential to the farm's daily operations. The reason is that the army needed food, and where else would they get their food from if not from farmers? Of course, in wartime, much of what the military eats are "MREs" (meals ready to eat) or "sea rations" as they are more commonly referred to. But even those processed meals begin with a harvesting of crops at a farm somewhere.

During that one-year waiver, I worked the family farm with the rest of my siblings, finished up the tenth grade, and tried desperately to get Essie to marry me. But on August 6, 1953, I became army property—government issue—a G.I. My parents drove me to the train station, where I boarded a railcar full of other drafted enlistees. It was a tearful farewell, as it was for most soldiers heading off to war. It didn't matter whether a soldier was black or white or brown or blue; one set of parents was just as worried as the other. It didn't matter that our destination was only Fort Jackson, South Carolina, just a few hundred miles east of our homes in

Tennessee and Mississippi. Our final destination would be Korea, where the communists were inflicting heavy casualties on American forces.

When we got off the train in South Carolina, our worlds instantly turned upside down. Suddenly, we had hardened men in green fatigues and brimmed hats screaming profanities at us and treating us like we were yesterday's garbage! As a black man reared in the South, I had heard some real gems. But what those men were calling the others and me that day, and for the next couple months, made southern bigotry seem like a conversation over tea and cookies! Back then, drill sergeants could still knock you around if you got out of line. Today, they aren't allowed to batter a recruit.

From Fort Jackson, where we picked up our military-issued uniforms and gear, we were transported to Fort Leonard Wood, Missouri, for eight weeks of Basic Combat Training (BCT). Missouri in August is hot and humid, and with all our combat gear on, it was just plain miserable. Not a day went by that we didn't march up hills with loaded rucksacks at least once, usually multiple times, since the post was located in the Ozark mountain range. They made sure to find as much mud for us to crawl through as they could, just so we didn't get spoiled. Still, most of us managed everything right. The daily physical training (PT) helped get us in shape for the long hikes, and the rifle training made us proficient marksmen.

Fort Leonard Wood was established in 1940 as a Basic Combat Training (now known as Initial Entry Training (IET) post in the build-up to America's anticipated involvement in WWII. But just a year later, the base expanded its mission by developing the Engineer

Replacement Training Center (ERTC), where combat engineers receive specialized training.

That's important because once I completed my Initial Entry Training at Fort Leonard Wood, I stayed to receive my Advanced Individual Training (AIT) as a combat engineer at the ERTC.

My advanced training as a combat engineer started just one week before Columbus Day, 1953. Capt. Greene, a sturdy 5'10" and pale as a glass of milk, was my commanding officer. His stern demeanor commanded respect, something I'll never forget.

After his new class of engineering candidates had all reported in, he called us to a formation on the parade field just outside of school. We stood at attention as Capt. Greene walked slowly up and down every row of recruits, scrutinizing each of us as if searching our souls for something specific. When he finished inspecting every soldier, Capt. Greene returned to the front of the formation, promptly telling us to stand at ease, which really meant parade rest (feet shoulder length apart, hands clasped properly behind the back). That's when I heard five words that made my heart leap within my chest.

"Private Hearn! Front and center!" Capt. Greene commanded. I must have hesitated because not more than a few seconds later, he hollered, pointing at the ground in front of his feet, "Are you deaf, Hearn? Now! Right here!"

I took a step backward out of formation before making my way around the platoon to stand before Capt. Greene, rigid as a board, eyes directed on his forehead. I had learned in basic training that looking an officer straight in the eyes when in trouble would get me double the punishment, so I was careful to look at Capt. Greene, but not directly in his eyes.

"At ease, Private Hearn," he said, his eyes memorizing every bit of me as he circled. "Where you from, Hearn?"

"Mississippi, sir."

"Is that right? Well, Mississippi," he uttered under his breath so only he and I could hear it, "I'm thinking you might be my new platoon leader. Any problem with that, Private Hearn?"

"Sir," I whispered, "I'm black. These fellers are all white. I don't think . . ."

"You let me worry about that, Private. For now, I want you to turn, bring them to attention, and then march them around the perimeter of the parade field and right back here. Understand me, Hearn?"

I thought about it for a short moment, then pulled myself to attention, saluted him, did an about-face, then hollered, "Platoon! Aaaattennnntion! Righhhhht Face! Forwaaaard march!" They began marching with me at their side, barking directions. I did just what Capt. Greene told me, bringing the platoon back to a stop in the same place as before.

"Platoon! Halt! Left face!" Then I about-faced, saluted Capt. Greene, who was just standing there grinning.

"Well done, Hearn. Dismiss the platoon and report to my office."

I reported as ordered, standing before him at attention as he wrote out something from behind his desk. Without looking up, Capt. Greene said, "Private Hearn, you are now in charge of my platoon."

"Sir," I said, "I really don't think. "

"You leave the thinking to me, Master Sergeant Hearn," he said, looking up to toss me an armband with a Master Sergeant insignia on it. "You wear this armband at all times. Anybody gives you any guff, handle it. Got it? You're in charge of the men."

"But, sir—"

Right then, he got up and came around the desk, placing a gentle hand upon my shoulder and looking me straight in the eyes. "I have faith in you, Son. You will do well. I'm sure of it. If you need help, you come to me."

That he, a white officer, called me, a black Private, "Son" was not lost on me. In fact, if I'm being honest, his affection had me all choked up. He could tell, I'm sure, but I doubt he knew why. After that, Capt. Greene walked me through everything I needed to know to be a great platoon leader. After the lesson, I returned to the platoon barracks. The men saw my new armband right off and the murmuring and head shaking began. But I didn't pay it any mind. Honestly, I think I was still in shock that this guy had the nerve to put a black man in charge of an almost all-white platoon when integrated Army units were still a relatively new phenomenon. I say almost because there was one other black man besides me; that's it. It didn't take long, however, for the men to realize they didn't have any other choice but to listen to me. I doled out weekend passes as well as punishment for infractions. If they wanted liberty, they had better not act up.

While all of this was happening, I still could not get Essie out of my mind. Only one week into my new platoon leader role, I went AWOL. Truthfully, I had granted myself an extended pass for the three-day holiday weekend, possibly celebrating Columbus Day, so I could return home to Mississippi and ask Essie to marry me. The problem was that I stayed home a couple days beyond my pass. Had Essie said yes, the risk of punishment would have been worth it, but as it was, Essie said no again.

When I got back to Fort Leonard Wood the following Wednesday, my attitude was lousy. Years of Essie's denial of me finally had taken its toll. I knew I would be disciplined for going AWOL, but I could not have cared less. I headed directly to Capt. Greene's office to receive my punishment, but was headed off by his second in command, a young second lieutenant whose name escapes me. The LT grabbed me by the arm and led me to a private area.

"Your bus broke down, right Private Hearn?" he said, nodding as if trying to get me to play along. "Right?"

"No, sir. I meant to make it back on time, but . . ."

"Yes it did, Hearn, you got me? That's what you're going to tell the old man." The "old man," of course, was his boss, Capt. Greene. "You know he likes you, Hearn. You being AWOL put him in a bad spot."

"I'm sorry, sir, but I can't do that," I said, looking him squarely in the eyes as if daring him to double up my punishment.

The LT stared me down for a long moment before turning to disappear into Capt. Greene's office. Minutes later, he reappeared, motioning with a sarcastic bow and wave of his arm for me to enter. I reported to the front of Capt. Greene's desk fired off a salute, and waited to be addressed. Without looking up, he said, "Take a seat, son."

I sat in a chair opposite his desk but sat at the position of attention, back straight, hands resting palm-down over my kneecaps, eyes directly ahead.

Capt. Greene looked up at me. "I've been good to you, haven't I, son?"

Once again, my throat constricted on the word "son." Something about a white man calling me son choked me up emotionally. I nodded in response. "Yes, sir, and I know I deserve to be punished for what I did."

"Who said anything about punishment, Hearn? I just wanted to know if I've treated you well?"

At that moment, I felt like crying. I felt like I had let my father down, not a captain in the United States Army. "Yes, sir. Very nice to me."

"Why'd you do it, then? You knew you only had a three-day pass. I put you in charge because I know you have a better head on your shoulders than that. Tell me why so I can understand."

Despite his order to tell him, I couldn't. It would have been too embarrassing. Instead, I shrugged as if to say, "I don't know."

"Well, you're right, Hearn, I do have to punish you for this somehow. What do you suggest I do to you?"

"I suppose you could send me to the stockade, give me an Article 15."
"Nope. Not going to do either. What else?"

"You could deny me passes or liberty for the rest of my stay."

"Not doing that either. Tell you what I will do, Hearn," he said, motioning for the lieutenant to bring over my master sergeant armband. "Stand up."

I popped up, at attention, of course.

He placed the armband on my right arm then stood before me. "*Now* you can salute me, Master Sergeant Hearn."

I fired off a disciplined salute.

"Listen to me now. Here's what you're going to do. You're going to dedicate yourself to leading my platoon to winning best platoon in the battalion. If you do, we're even. Your slate is clean."

"If we lose, sir?" I asked reluctantly.

With a wry grin, Capt. Greene replied, "You won't lose, Hearn. I have faith in you."

He was right. In the end, our platoon won. In addition, I ended up getting along really well with most of the guys, even though integration hadn't been a very popular notion; but then, change is hardly ever easy.

I remember an incident that happened after training ended that illustrates that point. Some of us had loaded a bus to travel from Missouri to Memphis, Tennessee. Once we crossed the Arkansas border, the driver pulled the bus to the side of the road, shut off the engine, and then stood and turned to face the passengers. He said, "All right, all you colored soldiers, move to the back of the bus."

I was tired and had my head leaning against the window, half in and out of sleep. The driver walked back to my row and said, "Wake that boy up."

I heard him loud and clear, and even though I didn't like it, I began to rise. Right then, the white soldier sitting next to me placed his hand on my shoulder, encouraging me to sit back down. Then he said, "Hell, no! He's not moving to the back. No."

The driver said, "Yes, he is. Get up, boy. Move."

That's when the white soldier, and for the life of me, I cannot remember that young man's name, stood eye-to-eye with the driver and said forcefully, "Driver, he's not moving to the back of the bus, so you might as well get back to driving."

I said, "It's all right. I don't want to start any trouble."

The soldier said, "I know it's all right. That's why you're not moving. This stuff stops now. Today, there isn't anybody moving to the back of the bus."

The two stared each other down for a long moment. I really thought we were about to have a fight, but the driver looked around at all the other soldiers, and I think he wisely realized that those other soldiers weren't going to let anything happen to their brother-in-arms, so he had better let it go. We rode the rest of the way to Memphis in the same seats we were in when we left Missouri.

That incident convinced me that the racial tides were shifting in America. Two years later, on December 1, 1955, on a commuter bus in Montgomery, Alabama, a woman would become the new face of Civil Rights when she refused to give up her seat to a white passenger. Her name, of course, was Rosa Parks, and later on, when I became mayor of Lancaster, California, I had the pleasure of meeting her. What a wonderful woman! She suffered many hardships for her act of defiance, including arrest and the loss of her job. But Rosa Parks pressed on. In the end, she inspired more than her own race; she inspired an entire nation.

This chapter reminds me that though there are people who would curse us or hurt us, so too are there those who want to love us and help us. The problem is that sometimes we cannot accept the loving grace being offered by some because our hands are full holding onto past hurt. We've got to go to the cross, kneel, and willingly lay our hurts at Jesus' bloody feet. Only then will we be able to rise and grasp the grace we want and need so desperately? It is this grace that God, through His children, holds out to us continuously.

CHAPTER ELEVEN

# DIVINE INTERVENTION— KOREA

By the time I arrived in Korea, the fighting had officially stopped. Only minor skirmishes continued between the North and South.

The Demilitarized Zone. More recently, North Korea's new dictator, Kim Jong-un, a mere boy at 29 years old, ratcheted up the threats against United States interests, to include nuclear proliferation of major western U. S. cities. Several years ago, his father, whom the young dictator recently succeeded, sank a South Korean battleship sailing in international waters off the coast of the Korean Peninsula. Both instances are a new reminder to the world that the peace agreed upon at the end of the Korean War is still as fragile as rice paper. At any moment, one wrong step by either side and the treaty might tear. It's not unlike many relationships between people, I suppose. Whether international, interdenominational, inter-political, inter-gender, or interracial, each requires tact, diplomacy, and grace to bear fruit.

In thinking about the dynamics of relationships, I'm reminded of a gentle soul I met on the long boat ride from Oakland, California to Yokohama, Japan, our first stop before going on to Korea. His name was Bob Johnston. Bob's kindness became a hallmark of his character. Just a kind young man with a heart for God! I remember him standing about 6'3" tall, thin as a matchstick, his blonde hair cropped short, and his skin a reddish-pale—kind of flush, like a white baby's skin, only Bob never outgrew his.

Shortly after our boat's departure from the West Coast of the U.S., I broke out my checkerboard. I loved playing checkers! And I was good, too! People would come by, take a seat opposite, spout some rhetoric about how they were going to smear me, and then promptly lose. Bob, always polite, meandered about for a couple days, watching intently, but never approaching. One day he got up the nerve and challenged me to a game. We got to playing and it didn't take long for Bob to start his spiel.

"Hearn," Bob said, "You play a fine game of checkers, I have to admit, but do you know the Lord? Do you have a personal relationship with Jesus Christ, Henry?"

I made my move, jumping and taking several of his checkers. "I know the Lord."

"I believe you," he said. "But do you have a personal relationship with Him?"

Now, I stopped and looked at him for a long moment. This young man had no desire to play checkers. He had only challenged me so he could share the gospel. A lot of guys would have told Bob Johnston to get lost, but something in me, perhaps the Holy Spirit, told me to listen. "I've been a believer most of my life, Johnston. My mama saw to that."

"I'm sure she did, Henry, but do you *really know* who Jesus is by the Bible?"

He had me. I hadn't really read much of my Bible over the years. I had learned what I'd learned from the preachers mostly, and from Mama and Great Grandpa Caruthers. I knew Jesus to be the Son of God.

And I knew that I was to trust Him—that He loved me. But I didn't really know Jesus.

Right then, Bob must have sensed my uncertainty because he reached into his bag and retrieved his Bible, worn like an old leather shoe that had gotten lots of use. He opened it to the Book of John, moved himself closer to me, and then walked me through the gospel as God had breathed it onto parchment. The next day, he took me down *The Romans Road*. The next day, another book, then another, until Bob was convinced I *knew* Jesus and what He had done for me on that cross at Calvary.

Those checkerboard Bible studies with Bob changed my life. I began to crave God's word. I started exploring my Bible the way God had intended— and it enriched my life tremendously. Here I am on my bunk in Okinawa, discovering God's word:

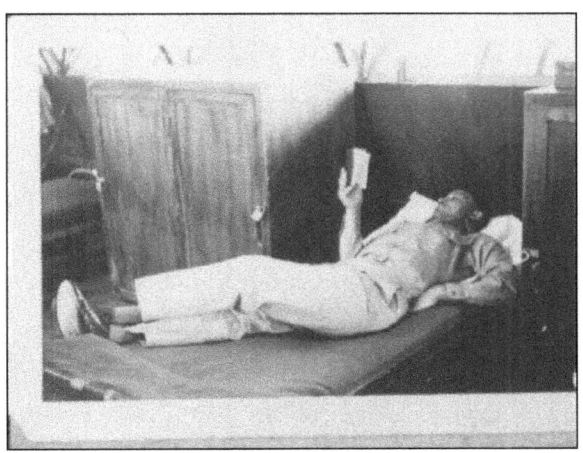

I don't know whatever happened to Bob Johnston. After we departed the boat in Yokohama, I never saw him again. I hope that if he's still alive and that he's doing well. I hope to see him again and thank him for taking the time to love me despite our different skin colors. I hope to impress upon Bob how important a role he played in my walk with God and my becoming a preacher because the more I came to know what God had done for me, the more I wanted to serve Him with my life. I owe that largely to Bob Johnston.

Once in Yokohama, Japan, we disembarked and were in-processed for departure to Korea. Part of that in-processing was the assigning of serial numbers to all soldiers and Marines, as well as duty assignments tied to each particular serial number. Once processed, we would board LSTs (Landing Ship, Tanks), which were smaller troop and equipment carriers designed to land on beaches, if necessary. But once again, God would intervene in my life, altering my future.

After the processing, two soldiers were without serial numbers or assignments—me and Billy, who also was black. He was also older and outranked me, having graduated from Tennessee State University, where he also played football. Billy decided that if the Army was dumb enough to forget about us, we might as well go enjoy ourselves in Japan, at least until they wised up and discovered the error. We didn't have a lot of money. After about two weeks, we grew tired of goofing off and reported back to the Army's in-processing center. We were worried that we'd face discipline for slipping out, but nothing happened except a verbal reprimand from the sergeant-in-charge and his commander. The way Billy figured it, they were stuck. It was their fault, and if anybody deserved formal punishment, they did. They had been negligent in their duties, not us. Of course, we had a duty to let them know about their mistake, but in our mind, that duty didn't have a time limit. We fulfilled our duty; we just took our time about it.

From Yokohama we caught an LST to Korea. Our first duty station was in Taegu, Korea, maybe 60 miles southeast of Seoul. We were assigned to the 808th Engineer Aviation Battalion (EAB). Few people know much about the Korean War, particularly the latest generation of Americans. For some reason or another, we as a country hardly discuss it in schools or in memorial celebrations, though it lasted three years and took the lives of over 30,000 American troops.[1] Perhaps that's why it's often referred to as *The Forgotten War*.

Taegu (later renamed Deagu) sat at the head of the Naktong River Valley, making it a vital route for North Korean advances against the South and the perfect place for the U. S. Eighth Army headquarters. Many battles were fought in and around Taegu, with American forces suffering heavy losses. Taegu became known for one of the more heinous events of the Korean War—*The Hill 303 Massacre*, in which 45 American mortar men from H Company of the 5th Cavalry Regiment, 1st Cavalry Division were captured, bound, and shot in the backs by North Korean troops. When American forces found them, their hands were still bound, bullet holes in their backs. A few survived to tell what had happened, prompting Gen. Douglas MacArthur to broadcast a warning to North Korean leaders that he would hold them accountable for the slaughter. *Time* magazine took the incident public.[2]

I got there in the winter of 1953, and it was brutally cold. The Armistice between the North and South had already been in effect for about five months and the fragile peace was holding. Still, a lot of work needed to be done, especially cleaning up the mess left from the shelling and fierce battles. All the while, we were very aware that war could easily erupt again.

Our job in Taegu was to tear down everything, pack it up, and have it ready to ship out when the time came. If we engineers could repair something, we would, but any damaged structures were usually demolished in the name of expediency. I'd say it took us approximately six months to

---

[1] U.S. Military Casualties – Korean War Casualty Summary, *Defense Casualty Analysis System*, United States Department of Defense (As of April 19, 2013), Retrieved April 20, 2013, https://www.dmdc.osd.mil/dcas/pages/report_korea_sum.xhtml
[2] Bell, James (August 28, 1950), "Massacre at Hill 303," *Time* ISSN 0040-781X

get everything squared away once we arrived. After that, we were sent to another post, this one in Kunsan, Korea, to do the same thing. Once that mop-up was complete, the Army reassigned Billy and me to Okinawa, Japan, where we would spend another year before returning home to our families.

Okinawa brought with it a more relaxing environment, and it was there that I first played the sport that would land me a college scholarship—football. Looking back, I find God once again at work in that whole experience. Had the Army not overlooked Billy and me during in-processing at Yokohama, we would have never met. I might never have gone to college at all. I would have likely returned home to work the family farm for the rest of my life.

Billy had played for TSU for three years, from 1950 to 1952, he turned out to be a great coach. Our battalion commander on Okinawa had heard about Billy's experience playing college ball and tasked him with forming a team to represent the battalion. Since Billy and I were friends, he resolved to have me play for him, teaching me everything he knew about the game. When the first sergeant relocated Billy's bunk from the platoon's Quonset hut to the sports equipment room (to keep watch over the battalion's sports equipment), he persuaded the first sergeant to let me go with him. That gave us ample time to discuss the nuances of the game. I became so good at playing football that Billy called his former coaches at TSU to tell them they had better take a look at me before another college got me. Here I am playing American football on Okinawa:

Now, rooming with Billy in the equipment room also gave us opportunities to influence each other in other areas of our lives. Billy was not really into the gospel, but I tried to share it anyway, praying all the while that God would open his heart to Christ's love. Billy, for his part, tried to get me to accompany him on his weekly excursions into town to be with the local women. I kept telling him that I wasn't into that, but peer pressure can be a daunting thing when you're in your early 20s, even for a young man grounded in the admonition of the Lord.

About halfway through our year in Okinawa, Billy finally persuaded me to go with him into town, the goal being to buy sex. I was still a virgin and felt torn about giving such a precious thing away in such a sleazy way. I can remember my mother telling me once that if I ever took advantage of a woman sexually, loving and leaving her, that I should not bother coming back home, that I would no longer be welcome in her home or as a son. I was bright enough to take her at her word. But did being overseas in a hostile environment negate Mama's stern warning? Billy's argument about being a man away at war had a skewed justifiability to it. Things could change at any moment, and who knew if we'd ever get the chance to have sex again, and sex is a right of passage for a young man (or so many are led to believe).

Billy dragged me to the village brothel with him, and we purchased a couple of young Japanese women, each obligated to spend an hour doing whatever the buyers wanted. Billy took his prostitute to his little room, and I took my prostitute to mine. Once in the room, she took a seat on the bed and waited for me to undress. But as I began to remove my clothes, the Holy Spirit shook my conscience loose from the grip of Satan, and I stopped. I asked her, "As beautiful as you are to me and to God, why would you sell yourself to me for money, letting me have my way with you and your body?"

She said sadly, "My parents were killed in the war between the United States and Japan, and I have to support my younger siblings. It isn't easy for me, but it is my responsibility."

I desired her. I won't lie about that lust or try to sugarcoat it. But I could not go any further. I had seen so much injustice perpetrated upon others by those who felt somehow entitled. Whether it is slavery or prostitution, what gets lost in the argument is duty. We have a moral duty to act on behalf of those in too weak a position to act for themselves. Don't believe me? Perhaps these words from the Apostle Paul will convince you: *"We who are strong have an obligation to bear with the failings of the weak, and not to please ourselves."* (Romans 15:1 ESV) Paul also said in Acts 20:35, *"In all things I have shown you that by working hard in this way we must help the weak and remember the words of the Lord Jesus, how he himself said, 'It is more blessed to give than to receive.'"*

At that moment, God had put it upon my heart to act on her behalf. Though she willingly sold herself to me, she could not have known the full ramifications of that action. I had a duty not to violate her in such a way.

I studied her for a long moment and then started gathering my things to leave. She panicked, and I said, "Please don't worry. I'm still going to pay you, but I'd like for you not to do this anymore, not to sell your body for sex. I promise you this: if you promise me that you won't sell your body anymore, I will support you and your two siblings for as long as I'm on Okinawa."

She began to weep, asking me why I would do such a thing for her. I said, "Because God cares too much for you, I care too much to see you do that to yourself. If it makes you feel better, you can come and clean my room a couple times each week at the field house."

She agreed, and I had the privilege of getting to know her and her younger brother and sister over the next six months. They even began attending church with me. For some reason, unbeknownst to me, the post chaplain had chosen me earlier to be his assistant chaplain. I remember when he selected me. I objected, telling him that I only had a tenth-grade education. He would not be dissuaded, however. Soon, I became his right-hand man, helping him prepare his schedule, filling out paperwork, and researching scripture for his sermons. That experience helped me draw nearer to God, and it also allowed for my new Japanese friends to give their lives to the Lord. Praise God for His divine planning! He sees it all and orchestrates our out-of-tune lives into beautiful symphonies! I do not know what became of those three siblings, but I do believe God put me in their lives at that moment to show them His love. Before leaving Okinawa, the eldest had given up prostitution and had found a small job of some sort on the Army post. I also made sure that the church staff on Okinawa would continue to encourage the young woman in her walk with Christ.

Before I close this chapter, I'd like to briefly discuss two other things that happened while overseas that impacted my life forever. The first was studying for and passing the GED exam so that if TSU offered me a scholarship, I'd qualify academically. The second thing will require a little more explanation but involved a boat ride home.

By the time I was slated to depart Okinawa for the United States, I had been promoted to corporal (seen in this photo), which is considered Non-Commissioned Officer (NCO) status. As such, the Army offered me a plane ride home rather than a boat ride, which would have shaved weeks off of my journey. Of course, I accepted, but just as we were set to board the plane, a sergeant who outranked me had taken my seat. I was livid! I cursed and threw a fit, cried racism and all of that, but there was nothing I could do except get in line with the rest of the soldiers for the boat ride home. A few hours later, while still waiting to board the boat, an announcement came over the loudspeaker that the plane had crashed en route, killing everybody on board.

Truthfully, I felt terrible inside. Of course, I was grateful to God for once again intervening in my life, but I was also sad for those who had lost their lives. That sergeant, unbeknownst to him, gave his life that I might live. That is a thought I have carried with me for some time now.

Perhaps it was this event, on top of all the other divine interventions that had happened up to that point, that finally convinced me God had a specific plan for my life. On the boat ride home, I thought hard about that, vowing to remain open to what God might call me to do for Him.

That incident with the plane reminds me of something else the Apostle Paul tells us, this time in Romans 8:28 (NIV): *"And we know that in all things God works for the good of those who love Him, who have been called according to His purpose."* We may not always like what God does for us, but we can trust that it is good and right and will work out in our lives according to His purpose. I didn't like being bumped from my spot on that plane ride home, but I'm alive today because it happened. I cannot say why God would choose me over another to live, but my sincerest hope is that I've honored that man's tragic death by being obedient to God's calling.

CHAPTER TWELVE

# RUNNING TO WIN THE PRIZE—TENNESSEE STATE UNIVERSITY

The boat shoved off from Okinawa, Japan, in early May 1955 for Oakland, California. From there, it was on to Camp Chaffey, Arkansas, for out-processing. On May 22, 1955, the Army honorably discharged me into my own care. That day, like many in my long life, will be forever etched in fondness. Only those who have served in the military will understand the sense of freedom and accomplishment that envelops your soul when you slip out of your uniform for the very last time and into a set of "civies" you've chosen especially for that day. There's a long look at your new self in the mirror, the turning out of your bed or barrack's room for the final time, and the walk outside, where you take in a deep breath of new beginnings before going merrily (or apprehensively) on your way, leaving the discipline of military bearing behind. You're now free to do as you choose and to be what you want to be. It feels terrific!

Somewhere along the way, the Army added an s to Hearn. My birth certificate spells it Hearn, but now it would be Hearns. I decided not to fight it.

In those days, the Army did not offer severance pay upon discharge, but they did have one of the greatest G.I. Bills in our nation's history. The G.I. Bill did not discriminate between races. It applied to all equally. My plan was to earn a spot on TSU's football team, hopefully with at least a partial scholarship attached, and then pay the remaining tuition with my G.I. Bill. But it would be a couple months before tryouts. That gave me time to go home and visit my family and to ask Essie for her hand in marriage one final time. If she said no this time, I would move on in life without her. To my honest surprise, however, Essie said yes.

Seeing Essie again made my heart flutter with joy, but her acceptance of my proposal made it sing out to the heavens! I rejoiced both inwardly and outwardly that God had answered my prayers! Our beloved parents were thrilled by the news as well. Henry and Essie were engaged! We hadn't set a date, but we were on our way!

During that time of re-acquaintance, I was also given the opportunity to establish the first football team for Hernando High School in Hernando, Mississippi, a city not far from our farm in Center Hill. Wow! Fifty-five years later and I can see it in my mind as if it were yesterday! I thoroughly enjoyed that experience and used it to help keep myself in football shape, knowing my tryout with TSU was approaching quickly.

Now, if you're a student of history, you know that the Civil Rights Movement in America was ramping up. In 1954, one year before I returned home from Korea and Japan, the Supreme Court of the United States ruled in *Brown v. The Board of Education* that blacks, by way of segregated schools, were not being afforded equal protection under the law as governed by the Fourteenth Amendment to the Constitution. This pivotal ruling set the stage for the integration of schools, much of it at the time forced integration. In 1956, the court's ruling was expanded to include all state-run schools. But that had nothing to do with my choice of attending Tennessee State University. TSU was an all-black university established during segregation so that Negroes, as we were called back then, could go on to higher learning. I chose TSU for one reason and one reason only—football. I tried out for the team and secured the offensive position of a right-pulling guard and the defensive position of nose guard.

They offered me a full scholarship. It was that simple. That scholarship was contingent upon my scores on the college entrance exam.

In August 1955, I walked onto Tennessee State University's football field and introduced myself to the coaches—Coach Keene (head coach), Coach Coffee, Coach Little (who was very big), and Coach Gentry. Coach Keene put a hand on my upper back and shoulders, giving a firm squeeze to see if I had a muscular upper body. I weighed about 210 pounds and was pure muscle.

"Billy called us, says you're quite a football player and that we should take a hard look at you," Coach Keene said. "All right, you seem pretty solid. We're going to put you through some drills. You pass, Hearns. You'll be all right. Now, show us what you've got. Do your best, Son."

Well, I must have done all right because I made the team, playing all four years on both offense and defense. I wasn't good enough to make it to the NFL, but I was good enough to start most games, and that suited me just fine. I loved playing football!

We had one of the best football programs around back then and one of the top teams. Grambling University in Louisiana held the number one slot, then TSU, then North Carolina A&T, and then the rest. We three schools beat the other schools day and night—just beat them all the time! It sure was fun playing for a team that won so often!

I must have done good enough on the college entrance exam because that fall, I began my coursework. In truth, I really had no idea what was considered a great score or a bad score. I didn't really care. All I cared about was whether or not my scores were good enough to play ball.

One day, while I was at practice, the vice-president of the university, Dr. Boswell, came down to the field. He called me over and said he wanted me to dine with him at his house that very night, directly after practice. I tried to make excuses for not going, like my clothes were not nice enough, but he insisted I come anyway. After the meal ended and it was just the two of us at the table, Dr. Boswell asked me why I had chosen to study agriculture. I explained that I had come to enjoy farming and everything that went with it, that I wanted to own a farm someday, just like my parents, and that I was sure I could pass all the classes. Dr. Boswell said, "Well, son, anybody can learn about agriculture, but there are some things that only a few can learn."

I said, "Yes, sir, but I like farming."

He said, "What I'm telling you, son, is that some people belong in agriculture, but you don't."

Well, I must have looked completely confused because he reached into a folder beside him and pulled out my official college entrance scores. He said, "Take a look at those. Tell me what you see."

I looked at the sheet and saw that the scores for mathematics and the sciences were very high compared to my English score. I said to Dr. Boswell, "Sir, these are not my scores. These belong to somebody else. I don't know anything about those things."

He said, "No, they are yours, Henry, and they show that you have an aptitude for math and sciences. Next semester I am going to teach algebra and I want you in my class. I'm going to tutor you because I believe you have a lot of potential to become an engineer." I hemmed and hawed a bit, trying not to disappoint him, but he finally said, "Henry, you really have only two choices. You can do this, or you can go home. No football. No degree from TSU."

I figured Dr. Boswell must have been under pressure from somebody higher up, perhaps the state or federal government, to start turning out black engineers. Understanding now how the allocation of government resources are distributed to government-run entities, and TSU was a state-run university, I'm led to believe that funds to the university were probably at stake if he did not comply. I suppose he did not give me the option because he had no options either. But, of course, that is pure conjecture at this point. From what I could tell about Dr. Boswell, he did not seem the type to willingly force a student's hand with regard to career choice.

Well, I took his algebra class and did excellent, just as he had predicted. From there, I went on to higher mathematics—trigonometry, calculus, and physics—and did well in all of them.

Now that I was enrolled in college and had secured my spot on the football team, I decided to make a few trips back to see Essie. Since we were now engaged, Essie began to draw closer to me. I wish we had waited until taking our nuptials to have sex—as God commands—but we didn't. That confession aside, Essie was the first girl I'd ever been with sexually, and I loved her with every ounce of my heart, even now after her 2008 passing.

We married December 31, 1955, during the break of my first and second semesters at TSU. Once we were married, Essie transferred colleges, leaving Russ College to come live and study with me at TSU. We didn't wait to have children. By the time we graduated TSU in 1959, we had two children, little Henry, and beautiful Valeria.

At first, Essie felt reluctant to let other students know we were married, and so we lived apart. But of course, once we started having babies, people took notice. We decided it was better to live like a normal married couple with children. We rented a room from a gentleman named Rev. Stockard. We supported our growing family on my GI Bill, leftover scholarship money, Army Reserve pay, and any work aid I had earned by doing odd jobs around campus. I had also saved about $3,000 while in the military, which at that time made for a healthy bank account. With that $3,000, I was able to pay for Essie's final years of college.

Now, when Essie had our first child—little Henry—she became very protective of him. She wouldn't let him out of her sight, nor would she let anybody touch him, rarely even me! But as our son got older, around the age of 2, I started to slip him out of the house by way of my duffle bag. I always carried a duffle bag with me when leaving the house, so there wasn't anything for Essie to be suspicious about. I'd lay him in my duffle bag on top of my clothes and books, tell him to be quiet until I say it is okay, and then slip out of the house. Essie would not know that her precious child was with me. That used to make her so mad! But I loved my boy too much to always leave him behind. I wanted my son with me whenever possible, even if that meant kidnapping him. Once we were far enough away from the house, I'd open my bag, pull him into my arms, and ask, "You all right, son?"

He'd say in the sweetest voice, "Yes, Daddy. Where we at?"

To him, it was fun, like hide and seek. Funny what some folks have to do to be with their kids. Eventually, Essie got wise to the game and would play along, acting like she didn't know, allowing me to think I was getting away with mischief. That's a fond memory for me. Sometimes, little Henry would just poke his head out of the duffle bag while it still hung from my shoulders, wrap his arms around my neck, smiling at passersby as we walked along.

Though my college experience at TSU brought great joy, many other black students at every level on the educational plane—particularly those students in the southern states—still suffered, fighting for their right to an education. One incident in particular, in the fall of 1957 (my third year of college), got the nation's attention. It happened in Arkansas and has become known as *The Little Rock Nine* incident.

Following the Supreme Court's ruling in *Brown v. The Board of Education*, the NAACP (National Association for the Advancement of Colored People), of which I'm a member, began enrolling willing black students into previously all-white schools. One such school was Central Little Rock High School in Little Rock, Arkansas. Nine black students enrolled to begin classes in the fall of 1957. Sadly, Arkansas's Democratic Gov. Orval Faubus called out the Arkansas National Guard on the first day of classes in an effort to block *The Little Rock Nine's* entry into the school. Faubus vehemently opposed giving blacks the same access to education as whites and stood prepared to use lethal force, if necessary, to stop it. President Eisenhower (Republican) sent in federal troops to enforce equal access and protection granted to all citizens, no matter their race, under the Fourteenth Amendment. The incident had the potential to incite another civil war. The entire nation watched on television to see how it would play out, even students at the all-black Tennessee State University.

On one side of the conflict were members of the United States Army's 101st Airborne Division, there to escort The Little Rock Nine into their new school. On the other side, members of the Arkansas National Guard were there to stop them in their tracks. Fortunately, Eisenhower was able to federalize all 10,000 members of the Arkansas National Guard, taking them out from under Gov. Faubus' control. Eisenhower's swift move put an end to the conflict, though many more would follow in the coming years at other schools across the nation.

Though I may have wanted to support my brothers and sisters in that fight back then, I felt God calling me to commit myself wholeheartedly to my growing family, my own education, and my walk with Him. Perhaps I would be able to help in the cause later, I felt, but not then. All I could do was pray for those on the civil rights battlefront—that God would convince the nation that it is better to love one another than to hate, to live in harmony rather than opposition.

I did get the chance and honor to meet Dr. King after hearing him speak at TSU the morning of February 21, 1956. His speech was entitled, *Going Forward By Going Backward*. No doubt Dr. King had a lot on his mind when he spoke to us. A grand jury had convened and was set to decide on whether or not to indict Dr. King and others for violating Alabama's boycott laws.

Dr. King had been one of 89 leaders to orchestrate the Montgomery Bus Boycott, a defiant yet nonviolent movement resulting from the arrest and conviction of Rosa Parks on December 1, 1955. Mrs. Parks wasn't the first to challenge Alabama transit laws. A black, 15-year-old high school student named Claudette Colvin had refused to give up her seat on a Montgomery bus just nine months earlier.

Colvin happened to be a member of the NAACP Youth Council, for which I now know—having had the chance to get to know Rosa Parks—Mrs. Parks served as an adviser. Young Colvin's arrest infuriated Parks and many others as well.

Dr. King and other civil rights leaders organized a massive non-violent bus boycott in hopes of bringing attention to the discriminatory practices of Alabama's transit system. When Dr. King's home was later firebombed, hundreds of angry blacks took to the streets in front of his burned-out home. In a remarkable show of restraint, Dr. King called for them to remain peaceful. I happened to come across Dr. King's calming speech that night and thought I'd share it with you here. His words still ring true today for every incident of hatred, whether racial or otherwise.

> *"If you have weapons, take them home; if you do not have them, please do not seek to get them. We cannot solve this problem through retaliatory violence. We must meet violence with nonviolence. Remember the words of Jesus: 'He who lives by the sword will perish by the sword.' We must love our white brothers, no matter what they do to us. We must make them know that we love them. Jesus still cries out in words that echo across the centuries: 'Love your enemies; bless them that curse you; pray for them that despitefully use you.' This is what we must live by. We must meet hate with love. Remember, if I am stopped, this movement will not stop because God is with the movement. Go home with this glowing faith and this radiant assurance."*[3]
>
> *—Dr. Martin Luther King, Jr. (1956)*

After he spoke to us at TSU, I got the chance to meet him briefly. He shook my hand and said affectionately yet authoritatively, "Hello, young man." Of course, I wasn't that far behind him in age; he having been born in 1929, me in 1933, but Dr. King still saw fit to address me as a young man. I'll never forget that. It seemed odd then, but looking back, Dr. King bore a heavy burden of responsibility, which I suppose must have

---

3 Darby, Jean (1990). Martin Luther King, Jr. Minneapolis: Lerner Publishing Group. pp. 41–42.

made him feel older. Even though Dr. King only spoke a few words directly to me, he has spoken volumes into my soul by his actions.

Like a lot of African American leaders in America today, I suppose I've tried to emulate Dr. King the most. I cannot recall another man — save Jesus Christ Himself and maybe Mahatma Gandhi (both of whom Dr. King himself tried to emulate)—who was able to effect unifying change through love, grace, and peace, forsaking violence and its corrupt offspring, hate, bitterness, and vitriol. I, too, have tried to use love, grace, and peace as unifying forces. Love, grace, and peace are sweet fragrances, pleasing the senses like flowers in a springtime bloom. Who doesn't like the smell of roses, or violets, or daffodils? Just as it's hard to turn your nose and gaze away from a bouquet of beautiful flowers, so too is it hard to turn yourself away from the beauty of grace, love, and peace.

One last thought before closing this chapter. I recognize that I was unable to participate in civil rights struggles at certain periods in my development as a man, but I do hope that I have honored with my whole life what was done by others in my stead. Hopefully, my life has been an example of the cause. The world in which we live can be a brutally ugly place. Jesus knew this better than anybody. He warned us of this time and again throughout the four gospels, but He also advised us on where to find love, rest for our weary souls, and peace, namely in Him. There is a time to fight, but that time may not be the same for each of us. Sometimes it is better simply to ignore that which is going on around us, focusing solely on the prize to come.

CHAPTER THIRTEEN

# THE SON SHINES, EVEN THROUGH THE CLOUDS OF SEGREGATION

## CALIFORNIA 1960–1964

Our senior year at TSU became a critical study period for both Essie and me. My course load and activity schedule jeopardized our ability to graduate on time. Something had to change.

I may have been able to handle my own commitments, but Essie had a heavy course load as well, and my commitments had begun to overlap too much with hers. We were not only students; we were also the parents of two young children who needed our attention. To remedy our dilemma, an agreement was made with my football coaches to do only the minimum practices and workouts. That would free up precious time needed to help care for the kids and to study more. Essie

and I would both need good grade point averages if we ever hoped to secure professional employment, and that reality became much more important to me than playing football. Looking back, it's hard to imagine us parenting two children, attending classes, studying, working, me playing football, and participating in other activities put on by my fraternity. We made it through with God's grace. He sustained us. It was not by our own might that we graduated but by His mighty hand. Praised be His name!

I walked with my graduating class in June 1959. Mama came, but my father chose not to attend. Daddy never did think much of higher education. But Mama was so proud! She rose up after I was handed my Bachelor of Science Degrees (a double major, one in Agricultural Engineering, the other in Civil Engineering) and yelled, "Thank you, Jesus!"

Her boy had graduated college, something she probably never thought would happen given Southern race relations at that time. I remember a banquet that was held for the football team. Mama came with me and was so nervous. Some of the guys on my team had well-educated, wealthy parents. Each player had an opportunity to introduce and say a word or two about his parents. After, the parents were given the opportunity to address the crowd. Well, Mama heard how articulate one man sounded, a doctor, I believe, and she leaned over to me and whispered, "Son, don't make Mama get up there and talk. I don't want you to be ashamed because Mama can't talk like that."

I said, "Mama, that doesn't make any difference." She said, "No, Son. Do not call me."

I said, "All right, Mama. I won't."

But as soon as they called on me, I just had to introduce the woman who had given me so much. Afterward, I violated my promise to her and asked Mama to say a few words. I know she felt unworthy somehow, but Mama ended up turning the place out! She spoke about Ada Dee McCrary, Mr. Burks, about sharecropping, and about how she would bring home

## The Son Shines, Even Through the Clouds of Segregation

burned-out light bulbs because we didn't know what electric lights looked like. And she related everything to the goodness of God. I will never ever forget that! I think I was prouder of Mama at that moment than she was of me. Others spoke, too, but Mama had become the main event. They loved her! What I remember most about my mother is that she was never one to shy away from proclaiming Jesus as Lord, a trait passed on to me. I have never retreated from believing and proclaiming that Jesus is my Lord and Savior. I'm not backing off of that for anybody.

After graduation, it became time to find work. There were few professional jobs being offered to blacks living in the South. Sadly, I would see signs posted for engineers, but when I walked through the door to apply, the positions had suddenly been filled. It didn't matter that the signs or postings would still be there for days and weeks after I left the building. "That position has just been filled" meant blacks need not apply. That left a lot of us wondering what to do and where to go to find work.

After failing to find employment in Mississippi or Tennessee, a few of us headed north to Motor City—to Detroit, Michigan. At that time in America, the auto business was booming. "The Big Three," as they were called—Ford, General Motors, and Chrysler—were turning out cars under so many different brands (Cadillac, Oldsmobile, Pontiac, and Chevrolet to name a few) that they had to have jobs for engineers. Once we arrived, however, we found the same unwelcome mat we had found in the South. We returned to our homes, dissuaded but not despondent. There was still hope and hope had made its home for centuries in the West.

With Horace Greeley's "Go west, young man!" repeating in our minds, Paul Conn, his wife, and I headed toward the setting sun, our hope firmly rooted in the Lord that He would provide opportunities for professional employment. Essie and the kids would join me later after I secured an engineering position and a place for us to live. Leaving them behind was hard. A part of me felt as though I was abandoning my family, but another part—the pragmatic and sensible part—knew the hardship of being separated would pay dividends later in a better quality of life together. Truthfully, though, California proved to be a difficult job market, as well.

Paul had a relative living in San Francisco. We headed there. Our plan was to bunk up together in the same room at his relative's home, minimizing expenses until at least one of us found work that could support the group. It's a good thing we knew each other well because I ended up sharing the same bed as Paul and his wife, them at one end, me at the other.

I remember one day, after having had no success at finding employment, approaching a man I saw sitting on his front porch. He was white, a pleasant sort of fellow, and didn't seem to mind me approaching up his driveway. When I got close enough, I asked him if he might possibly hire me to do some yard work. I humbly explained my situation, that I had graduated college and had come out to California to find work, leaving my family behind in the process. I explained that I missed my wife and kids and wanted to earn some money somehow to bring them out to California. Well, he thought about it and said, "I'll tell you what, young man, I'll hire you today if you would be willing to tear down an old shed I've got in my backyard. And I'll pay you good money . . . $60 if you're interested. I'm just tired of looking at the rickety thing."

*Sixty dollars!* I thought. "Sir, you got yourself a deal. I have a friend that will help me, and we'll have it done by the end of the day."

Sixty dollars was a considerable sum back in those days, especially for demolishing a small shed. I went and got Paul, and we tore that shed down so fast! When we brought the man outside to get his approval, he stood there impressed, looking at the lumber from the shed stacked and bundled in neat piles, all debris raked, swept, and picked up. We left a dry patch where the shed stood.

He said, "That's great work," as he handed us $60. "Here's the 60 I promised. I know it's not enough to get your family out here, young man, but hopefully, it will help a little."

We said goodbye to the kind man and went on our way, happy that we finally had a little good fortune in our pockets. Not long after that, we came across an announcement that United Airlines was hiring in San Francisco for airplane washers. No, it wasn't the professional positions we had hoped for, but they were paying good money, and if we were lucky enough to secure one of those positions, we would at least be able to support ourselves while looking for the type of work we wanted.

We went over to United Airlines and got in the long line of applicants, Paul in front of me. When Paul got up to the window, the guy accepting and reviewing the applications saw that Paul had a college degree and refused his application, telling Paul he was over-qualified. Well, I heard that and got out of line to ask for another application. I decided I would not list my engineering degree but only that I had one year of college coursework. When I got up to the window, the guy looked over my application and hired me. But in my mind, I knew that I had lied to get the job, and my conscience began eating at me. I kept hearing Mama's voice telling me, "Never lie or steal, no matter what happens," a sentiment impressed upon me with a switch after I had stolen that boy's toy truck as a kid.

So now, bearing the weight of what I had done to get the job, I told Paul I had to tell them the truth. Paul said, "If you don't get this job after confessing, don't think you're going to be sharing that bed with me and my wife anymore. We need money, man."

I said, "Paul, I have to tell them the truth."

He said, "You take your chances, partner. But remember, you will not be staying with us at my uncle's if this goes badly. You got yourself a job, which will help support us all until I can get a job. That was our agreement."

But I had lied and knew confession was in order. Carrying un-confessed sin around is like standing on the platform of life with a noose around your neck. The more un-confessed sin you carry, the heavier you become until one day, the floor collapses underneath you, choking all life out of you. Rather than being dead *to* your transgressions when "made alive in Christ" (Ephesians 2:5), you become dead *in* your transgressions once again.

I got back in the line, which was considerably shorter by then, and the man said to me, "Mr. Hearns, didn't I already hire you?"

I said, "Yes, sir, but I wasn't telling the truth about my education. I put down that I only have one year of college, but the truth is I have my Bachelor of Science degree in Civil Engineering and Agricultural Engineering if I'm being totally honest. I double majored."

He said, "I see. Well, let me ask you this. Would you be willing to take our aeronautical engineering exam?"

Here, I had lied, and now he was offering me another opportunity—a better opportunity. I told him, "No, sir, because I won't pass the test. I know nothing about aeronautics."

He said, "What have you got to lose? Why not at least try? You might do better than you think."

After careful thought, I agreed. He put me in a room by myself with the test booklet and scratch paper on the desk before me. I looked down at the test booklet, scanned over the questions, then thought to myself, *There is no way I can pass this test. This is all foreign to me.*

But I tried anyway, looking at each question logically. It took me approximately an hour-and-a-half to do the first three questions. After the first hour-and-a-half had passed, something strange happened that I cannot explain and most will find hard to believe. Still, it's true nonetheless. Right then, as I was about to give up, a set of strong hands wrapped around my big head, fingers locked together for a strong grip. I could still see, though. It felt like my body had been set on fire. Honestly, I was scared to death! I hadn't seen or heard anybody come into that room, but somebody entered somehow.

My reaction was to reach up and grab the hands that were assaulting me, but when I tried to lift my arms, they met with what seemed like a metaphysical resistance, an invisible force. My forearms and hands wouldn't go high enough to pull the foreign hands from my eyes and head. I started wondering if I might be having a stroke or some sort of paralysis. That's when a voice said to me, "Write the answers I give you.

A. C. All of the above—"

Once all questions had been answered, the hands disappeared. I jumped up, turning quickly to catch my assailant before he left the room, but I stood there alone. The experience rattled me deeply. After taking a long moment to gather myself, I went to turn in my exam. The man I met before asked me to wait while he graded my test. When finished, he called me back over to him. He said, "How do you think you did?" I said, "I don't know."

He said, "You only missed three. That's it. Not bad for somebody who doesn't know anything about aeronautics."

Confused, I said, "That can't be. I guessed at all but the first three."

He grinned and then showed me my paper. The three questions I missed were the first three, the ones I tried to reason on my own. Even now, 50-plus years later, I still do not know what happened in that room while taking the aeronautical engineering exam for United Airlines. All I know is that something paranormal aided me. I'll leave it to you to decide whether or not it was God. I only know that without any help from that being, I would not have passed that exam.

To make a long story shorter, they hired me on the spot, though I was nervous that I wouldn't be able to perform the functions of an aeronautical engineer. That Monday I arrived at work and was instructed to visit every department at United Airlines to learn what they did, and that's what I did for some time, just learning how each department operated. Then, they assigned me briefly to a tool and parts crib where I would quickly learn each airplane part. While that was going on, however, one of the other companies to which I'd applied called me in for an interview.

The company was located in San Fernando, California, about seven hours south of San Francisco, and they wanted me for a civil engineering position. I thought hard about the choice I had to make. United Airlines had given me a wonderful opportunity, and I was about to throw it away. United even wanted to send me to school on a full salary, but I turned it down, opting instead for the civil engineering position in Southern California. In the end, I suppose my concern about actually being able to perform the essential functions of an aeronautical engineer got the better of me. Passing the exam was one thing, but doing the job—one that could cost lives if I failed—was something entirely different. But United Airlines wouldn't let me off so easily. They wanted me to stay on with them, even offering me more money and incentives. Perhaps they saw promise in me. Perhaps they were being led by a desire for ethnic diversity in their professional-level workforce. I'll never really know for sure. All I know is that I had been schooled in civil engineering and that's where my heart and interests truly rested. The money and incentives, oddly enough, did not matter.

The money I'd earned while at United Airlines allowed me to initiate the relocation of Essie and the kids to California. I missed them all dearly. Little Henry, whom we called "Buddy," was pushing 5 years old, Valeria, my sweet daughter, approaching 2 years old, and Theodore, whom we

## The Son Shines, Even Through the Clouds of Segregation

would later call "Hugo," was due to deliver in just a couple months. They needed their daddy, and I needed them. But I also needed Essie close to me again. Nothing calmed my senses like Essie's presence, her playful wit and intoxicating laugh, and her gentle affections. I cannot tolerate being apart from my beloved family. Not then, not ever.

I started work for the Soil Conservation Service in the latter months of 1960, and I quickly realized an ill-tempered man who did not like Negroes or coloreds, as we were sometimes still called, ran the San Fernando office. Looking back, I sometimes have to chuckle to myself (in between the tears) at the silliness of racism. It reminds me of a quote I came across recently by Bert Williams, a Vaudeville-era comedian. Williams said, "It's no disgrace to be colored, but it's awfully inconvenient." That any race, whether white, black, brown, or olive-skinned, whether Jew or gentile, African or Asian, would consider themselves superior to a race of a different color, ethnicity, or origin is illogical and, like I said, silly. Are we not all God's children? Were we not all made in His image? Did God not send Christ to die on that cross for each of us?

I arrived in San Fernando a day early so I could locate the place without regard for a time clock. The day was Sunday, and when I found the building, to my surprise, there was somebody inside. I knocked on the window to get the man's attention, but he just looked at me and kept doing what he was doing. I knocked again, this time holding up my reporting document given to me by the main office in Santa Barbara, California, upon my hiring. This time, the man came over, opened the door, and said coldly, "We don't work here on Sundays, feller. Can't you see that?" Then he slammed the door and left me standing there.

I thought to myself, *Oh no. I sure hope this isn't my boss.*

Monday morning came and I reported to a very nice woman who turned out to be the secretary for my boss. She said, "Have a seat here, Mr. Hearns. The boss will be in shortly."

While waiting in the front area for "the boss" to arrive, an older gentleman, already hard at work, walked up and introduced himself. "So you're Mr. Hearns. My name is Joseph. I'm the soil conservationist here. Let me be the first to welcome you! We're so glad to have you on our team."

I thought, *Wow! I sure hope this is my boss.*

He said, "I trust you found a place to stay okay in town? After you see the boss, I'd like for you to come see me in my office."

His words let me know that he was not my boss, leading my gut to once again turn with worry. A few minutes later, the same man from the day before came through the door, the secretary trying to introduce me as he breezed past, on his way to somewhere more important, no doubt. A few seconds later, *Slam*! I presumed the noise to be his office door. The woman stopped at the door, took a deep breath, and then went in to see him. Within a few minutes, she returned, motioning for me to follow her back to the rear drawing room, past the other engineers, each of whom had been given office space.

Her face turned red from embarrassment when she pointed out my desk. "I'm sorry, Mr. Hearns. It appears that this will be your office for now. Please understand . . .

## The Son Shines, Even Through the Clouds of Segregation

"It's all right," I said. "I'll make the best of it."

She cleared off a drawing table in a room already stuffed to capacity with drawings and politely asked if she could get me anything. I shook my head, no, and she left the room.

A short time later, after I got my desk situated, the boss came in to see me, hands full of drawings that he promptly dropped onto my tabletop-desk. He said sternly, "I want these drawings reviewed and back to me by Friday morning." Then he turned and stormed out.

I rose and followed, trying to get his attention, but when I got to his office, he slammed the door in my face. I stood there for a moment, my nose catching a whiff of the wood-stain used on his door, wondering if leaving United Airlines might have been the biggest mistake of my life.

On my way back to my drawing room office, Joseph, the older gentleman I'd met earlier, called me into his office, motioning for me to close the door and sit down. He said to me, "Mr. Hearns, I'm afraid that San Fernando is a racially prejudiced city."

This was way back in 1960. It's changed for the better since then.

"I'm sad to say that there are no Negroes living in San Fernando," he continued. "The closest city with a welcome mat would be Pacoima, I'm afraid. Have you found a place yet?"

I said, "No, not yet."

Joseph took out a newspaper and spent a few minutes of his time helping me look for rental listings in Pacoima, helping me to find a rental house that very day. Since I didn't have a car either, he offered to run me around town until I could buy one. Had it not been for my kind colleague taking an interest in me, I might very well have called United Airlines to see if they would take me back. But as has always happened in my life, whenever bigotry revealed itself in one person, like in my new boss, love and, grace, and generosity revealed themselves in another.

After receiving such an overwhelming amount of drawings at one time, and since I hadn't quite learned what was meant by "review these drawings," I called my friend, Ralph Williams, in Los Angeles. Ralph had graduated from TSU just a year earlier than me and had taken a job with the L. A. County Department of Water and Power. The following night,. Tuesday, I went over to his house, and we spent the entire night reviewing and marking up those drawings. Wednesday morning, after a sleepless night, I turned in those drawings to my new boss, proud that I had delivered them two days earlier than asked.

Of course, the boss took great delight in crushing whatever pride I'd felt. He grabbed his red pen and began marking out many of my corrections and suggestions, berating me the entire time. "Stupid. Ignorant. Laughable. I would expect a grammar school child to know more than you—more than this dumb sh—" It went on and on until he handed the drawings back to me. "Try again, boy."

His vitriol did not phase me, however. In fact, I had expected it. He obviously didn't want me working for him, but I wasn't going anywhere. I'd seen worse treatment than that over the years. The next day I had those drawings exactly how he wanted them. I had learned how he scrutinized certain things and how he preferred others. From that day forward, I gave him very little to gripe about.

My tenure with the Soil Conservation Service lasted seven long years. During that time, I polished my skills and became a sought-after civil engineer. I even designed a couple bridges for the city. One day, after a bad rainstorm, my bigoted boss came into my office asking if I had gone out like he had told me and checked the integrity of my bridges to make sure they had held up the way they were supposed to against inclement weather. Without going into all the engineering mumbo jumbo about hydraulic water flow and such, I told him I had and that everything looked great. But I did confess that there was one area I couldn't get to because of excess mud. That confession was all the excuse he needed to lay into me. He called me every insulting name in the book, making up a few doozies, too! "Hearn," he screamed, "you stupid #@!* . . . #@!* . . . #@!*! When I tell you to do something, do it!"

You know, for the first time in my life I lost sight of reality and reached across my drawing table and grabbed him by the neck, pulling him to me over the tabletop. I think I said something like, "Don't you ever, ever talk to me like that again! You got me? I've done had enough of that kind of talk!"

Truthfully, I could have released 25 years of pent-up frustration in that momentary burst of anger, but I chose mercy. I could see he was about to choke out of consciousness, and I let him go. Once released, he stormed out. I thought for sure he had gone to call the police, but I wasn't afraid. I was just mad, more at myself than him.

Well, I waited and waited and the police never did come. Later in the day, my boss returned to the drawing room where my desk was located. But he did not enter right away. He stood outside the door, tossing his straw hat onto my table-desk. It took only a second for me to recognize the hat and I swiped it from my desk onto the floor.

A few seconds later, he poked his head inside and said, "I guess it's safe to come inside now. My hat didn't come back to me in pieces." He went on as he approached, saying, "I'm told preachers forgive." He had heard that I had done some preaching while I was in college. "I need to talk to you, Henry. I was born and raised in Watts. I was one of the only whites and got treated awfully bad by Negroes. I swore that I would never have one work for me. Never. But you defied my intent. You came highly recommended. In fact, the head office forced me to hire you. I did not want you because of how I had been treated by blacks in Watts, but you've been different from day one. I didn't want to believe that a black man could be like you, but now I know I've been wrong, and I need you to forgive me."

Needless to say, his confession blew me just about out of my shoes. I thought about what he had said, about how similar our experiences were growing up, only reversed. I said somberly, "Yes, preachers should forgive, and I confess that I've not acted like a preacher today. I hope you can forgive me as well."

That happened sometime in year five, if I recollect correctly. After that, we were all right. We became friends, sometimes sharing with each other our experiences with prejudice. I stayed for another two or three years before leaving to take a position at Edwards Air Force Base, just a couple hours northeast of San Fernando.

I learned a very important lesson from that experience at the Soil Conservation Service. There can be no bondage in forgiveness, but many wonderful bonds can form out of forgiveness.

CHAPTER FOURTEEN

# "OH, LET US EXALT HIS NAME TOGETHER!"

There has perhaps been no greater call on my life than to serve God and His flock as a pastor. But before I can elaborate on my 48 years of experience, I need to share with you another peculiar incident that happened to me while at Tennessee State University. It defies belief and set about changes in my course.

In 1958, during my junior-senior year at TSU, I was attending Fifteenth Avenue Baptist Church in Nashville. At that time, I participated in work-study. My job was to clean the university's administration building. My responsibilities included keeping watch over the keys during my shift. But one night, after finishing my work and locking up, those keys mysteriously disappeared from my pocket.

I had taken my son boating and had lost the keys either enroute to the lake or on the way home. That meant the entire administration building would have to be re-keyed, and I'd likely be fired. I frantically searched everywhere for those keys but with no success. They were long gone. I returned home and tried to sleep, thoughts swirling of what I would say to my supervisor the next day. In the middle of the night, the Lord stirred me awake. I heard His still, small voice whisper to me, "Do you remember that promise you made to Me in 1953 before you went to Korea, that if I got you home safely, you would serve Me with the rest of your life?"

I thought my mind had forsaken me! Was it really God, or was it my conscience eating at me over un-confessed sin, the sin of not fulfilling a promise I had made to God? I uttered softly so Essie couldn't hear, "Yes, Lord. I remember. I did promise that to you. I'm so sorry I haven't been faithful."

Then God said to me, "Henry, I will show you exactly where those keys are if you honor that promise to Me."

I said, "Okay, Lord."

He said, "Go back to the lake."

I protested, saying, "I've already scoured that entire shore of the lake, Lord. The keys are not there."

He said, "Yes, Henry, they are there, and I'll lead you right to them."

I rustled myself out of bed, still thinking I might be crazy, slipped on my clothes, and out the front door, following God's lead all the way back to the lake where I had taken Henry Jr. boating. Once there, God led me to an exact spot on the shoreline before telling me, "Wade out. Go straight until I tell you to stop."

I removed my shoes and rolled up my trouser legs, my eyes searching the darkness around me for curious onlookers. Thankfully, there were none. I began my short trek through the water, making my way toward the center of the lake. When I got to where the water was just knee-high, I heard, "Stop. Reach your hand into the water and retrieve your keys, Henry."

"Okay, Lord," I said, sinking an arm into the water. When my fingers touched the muddy bottom, I felt the coldness of metal. The keys! I yanked them out with such ferocity that I splashed myself in the face. "Well, I'll be!"

During the walk home, my mind pondered God, His desire for me to serve Him, and, of course, how it was that my keys ended up in the lake.

*"Oh, Let Us Exalt His Name Together!"*

Once inside the house, I returned to our bedroom and woke Essie. I asked Essie if I actually had keys in my hand. She looked at me with a cockeyed stare, eyes half-worried, half-irritated, and then said, "Is there something wrong with you? Seriously? You wake me up to ask me if those keys are really keys? Really? What else would they be, Henry?" When I didn't answer, Essie added, "You're scaring me, Henry. Go to sleep."

In the following days, I went to see Pastor Cornell at Fifteenth Avenue Baptist Church. We spoke about what had happened with the keys and the promise I had made in 1953. He told me he had been watching me for some time, how others looked up to me and sought me out for guidance. He impressed upon me that God had given me a gift and that to not give it back to God in service would be failing Him and His children. Within a few weeks of that conversation, I gave my first sermon. I preached from Ecclesiastes 12:1 (NIV)—*"Remember your Creator in the days of your youth."* My sermon title was, "Don't go too far and don't stay too long."

God had gotten my attention, for sure! From that moment forward, I knew my future would include preaching. The problem for me was that I wanted to be an engineer. Yes, God had blessed me with the gifts of service and preaching, but God had also blessed me with a mechanical aptitude. Surely, He had a purpose for giving me that as well.

This conflict between what we want for ourselves and what God wants for us has been happening since the Garden of Eden. God calls those who shun His desire *a stiff-necked people*. It is human nature to be stiff-necked and stubborn, but it is also folly. Read the words of King Hezekiah in 2 Chronicles 30:8-9 (NKJV): *"Now do not be stiff-necked, as your fathers were, but yield yourselves to the Lord; and enter His sanctuary, which He has sanctified forever, and serve the Lord your God, that the fierceness of His wrath May turn away from you. For if you return to the Lord, your brethren, and your children will be treated with compassion . . . for the*

*Lord your God is gracious and merciful, and will not turn His face from you if you return to Him."*

I had always felt God's hand upon my life, and in almost everything, I've tried to be obedient. What I mean by "almost" is after graduating college and relocating to California, I put away the promise to serve God and focused for a time on serving myself, pursuing my engineering dreams with little regard for the promise I had made to God. Sure, I taught Sunday school and tried to stay involved in my local church, but it wasn't the commitment I'd offered God—the one He'd accepted from me. To get me back on track, God brought a prophet of sorts into my life to challenge me with a single question.

We had been in California for a year or two, and my career as an engineer was beginning to take root. I had also established our membership in the Greater Community Baptist Church in Pacoima, a church pastored by the Rev. T.G. Pledger. My family attended faithfully while I taught Sunday school. Still, we were renting rooms out of a woman's house in Pacoima— Gloria was her name—while we waited for escrow to close on our first house. Gloria's father pastored a church back east somewhere and had come to visit his daughter. One day, he and I found ourselves alone in the house. We began talking about this and that, getting to know a little about each other. Suddenly, he looked me in the eyes and said, "Son, what are you running from?"

"Sir?" I said, unsure what he meant.

"You seem like a nice young man, but you're running from something. I can see it in your eyes and hear it in your voice. So what is it?"

I said, "No, sir. I work as an engineer during the daytime and wash dishes at a restaurant up on Sierra Highway during the evenings. I'm just trying to make a living so I can give my family a good life."

He said again, "Yeah, but you *are* running from something. Are you running from preaching, son?"

*"Oh, Let Us Exalt His Name Together!"*

Right then, my gaze lowered to the floor, the weight of conviction heavy. I said, "I guess maybe I am. I feel a calling to preach, but Essie never wanted to be a preacher's wife, and I've always wanted to be an engineer. That's one of the reasons why I came out here to California, to get away from preaching. If I'd stayed back in Tennessee, that's where I was heading."

He said, "Son, you need to go tell your wife that God is calling you to be a preacher and that you aren't going to run from it any longer. Whatever she does with that is her decision. Tell her you love her and want her with you, that you will treat her with the utmost respect always, but that you sense this is God's will for your life. After that, go and confess your calling to your pastor, see what doors open up."

Well, after a few days of working up my courage, I confessed to Essie that I had been harboring a secret—that God had called me to preach and that I had been wrongfully suppressing that calling. I informed her that if an opportunity to preach presented itself, I would need to carefully consider it. She voiced her objections and concerns, of course, noting that we had just purchased our first home and that we were now parents to five young children, but ended the conversation by saying she would support me in my decision to the extent that she could.

I had been teaching Sunday school for about four years at Greater Community Church by the time 1965 came around. During that four-year span, I went through the process of being ordained. After ordination, they made me an assistant pastor. Shortly thereafter, I preached my first California sermon, preaching several more over the next few months. Had God seen fit to have me preach only intermittently, I would have been satisfied. But God had bigger plans for me.

Before I go on, let me say this: sharing God's word with others came as natural to me as making honey does to a bee. And it sure enough tastes sweet on my lips like honey! I just love the word of God! When I think that I'm reading and speaking the words of our Creator, of the One who spoke the world into existence and who formed man and woman from the dust of the earth, I am in awe. Sometimes I just want to shout from the rooftops: *"Oh, magnify the Lord with me, and let us exalt His name together!"* (Psalm 34:3 NKJV) That the God of Life would entrust me, a black man born to uneducated sharecroppers in the segregated South, to teach His holy word is nothing short of astonishing. I am privileged beyond measure to have been given such a gift.

In March 1965, after delivering my third or fourth sermon as interim pastor of another church called First Missionary Baptist Church of Littlerock, California, a vote was taken by the church to appoint a permanent pastor. I thought the vote was for a permanent, *interim* pastor since the deacons had several of us filling in for the previous pastor, who had moved to Texas. To my surprise, they voted me in as senior pastor (*the* pastor).

At that time, First Missionary Baptist was a small church and occupied about an acre of rural desert landscape one hour north of the San Fernando Valley, where Pacoima was located. The congregation couldn't have been larger than 40 people and they were in desperate need of full-time, permanent shepherding. But, not all the deacons were on board with my appointment. A few threatened to leave if I was hired. Still, the majority was in my favor, and I was offered the position.

Well, I could not accept the position without first discussing the opportunity with my wife. I brought the subject up after dinner one evening after the kids had gone to sleep. Essie was not as thrilled about the offer. By then, we had moved into our first home and had begun building our life together in Pacoima. Essie said, "I'm not moving. You do what you want, Henry, but we've made this our home, and the kids and I are staying put."

That put me in a bit of a dilemma because I felt in my heart that God was calling me to pastor that small desert church. He also called me to shepherd my family. I knew Essie meant business when she said she and the kids would not join me if I moved up to the high desert. I decided to accept the position, but on the condition that I could commute from Pacoima. This seemed doable to me because the congregation at First Missionary Baptist Church was small enough to be led on a part-time basis. I could drive up a few times during the week for meetings and Bible studies after getting off of work at the Soil Conservation Service. I would be there on Sunday mornings for the service. All seemed to be going well for a time. I say "seemed" because while I was building up the church in Littlerock, my marriage was beginning to crumble. I'll talk more about that in the following chapters. For now, I would encourage you to submit in total obedience to the Lord if you hear His calling, even if contrary to your own desires, knowing that God will surely bless your commitment. Remember, the yoke of God's good and perfect will is easier to bear than your own stiff neck.

CHAPTER FIFTEEN

# RESURRECTED IN CHRIST

Part of the human condition is that we are prone to feelings of inadequacy from time to time. This unfortunate occurrence infects even the most celebrated champion at one time or another. It is what those competitors do to lift themselves that makes them champions. It has been said in one variation or another that most people quit just before they meet with success or that things seem to get hardest just before we accomplish what we've set out to do. I, too, have suffered through the desire to quit before God could finish His good work in me.

In the mid-to-late 1960s, we were still living in Pacoima, though I had begun commuting to the church in Littlerock, where I was pastor. Essie and I were having marital problems by then but trying desperately to work through them. The biggest issues facing our holy union were my ambition and my growing commitments up in the high desert—away from Essie and the kids.

I had been pastor of First Missionary Baptist Church for about three years when an incredible job opportunity came my way. I had come across a job announcement for civil engineers at Edwards Air Force Base, California, just a 30-minute drive from my church in Littlerock, and knew I had to apply. Edwards was and still is home to the Air Force Flight Test Center, the NASA-Dryden Flight Research Center and the Air Force

Rocket Propulsion Lab. I'll talk more about the base's rich history in the next chapter, but just so you understand why this opportunity was like no other, each of these three institutions played a vital role in our nation's space exploration program and in the world's understanding and progression into supersonic and hypersonic flight.

Edwards AFB, especially during the 1960s, 70s, and 80s, was an exciting place to be, a place where only a select few were granted access.

Accepting the job at Edwards AFB meant that I would need to relocate my family from Pacoima to the High Desert area known as the Antelope Valley. Essie, however, did not like the windy and barren desert and refused to move. We were at an impasse. I began living out of my church office— sleeping on a cot and showering at the base gym before going to work—so I could meet the daytime demands of my new job and the weekday-evening demands of my pastorship. As foolish and selfish as it may have been, my thinking was that Essie would begin to miss me like I missed her, eventually caving to the idea of relocating to the Antelope Valley. But instead, Essie started thinking the worst, that I had begun sleeping around with other women. In reality, I was as faithful as ever, just struggling to meet all my responsibilities, which at that time were so spread out geographically.

I understood why Essie did not want to leave our home in Pacoima to move to Littlerock, but families are meant to be together. Perhaps I shouldn't have accepted so much responsibility so far from home, but I felt both the pastorship and the engineering position at Edwards AFB were God-given opportunities, and felt a duty to accept them both.

I pleaded with Essie to drive up for the late-evening church meetings so that her mind would be put at ease. She refused, threatening divorce instead.

I cannot express how brokenhearted I felt at that moment. Honestly, I did not want to live anymore. Essie was the only woman I had ever wanted. From the moment I laid eyes on her at 16 years old, when I knocked on her door for a drink of water, I loved her. Without her in my life, it wasn't worth living anymore. The only question was how to end it.

One night, on the side of a pitch-black Sierra Highway, a rural mountain road that linked Los Angeles to the Antelope Valley (Lancaster, Palmdale, Littlerock, Sun Village, and many small townships), I stopped my car, got out, and thought it over. I was out in the middle of nowhere. My eyes began searching the night for some way to commit suicide. That's when I heard a distant train horn. That was it. I would throw myself in front of a speeding train, and my life would be over. It sounds so irrational now, even dramatic, but that's how I felt at that moment—despondent and alone.

I climbed a small cliff near the railroad tracks, looking for a perch from which to jump once the train barreled down on my location. It was dark outside and not much moonlight, at least at the lower levels, so the climbing was treacherous. But I really didn't care if I fell or jumped. I only hoped that if I fell, it would do the job. Once I found a good location from which to leap, I waited. That's when the most frightening thing happened; it could only have come from God.

The hands of my watch glowed in the dark, and as I watched the second hand tick, I felt an odd peace. Odd because it amazes me that any man could be at peace with killing himself, with willingly abandoning and traumatizing his beloved children for purely selfish reasons. Still, at that moment, I thought of nobody but myself. In just a few minutes, when that chugging hunk of steel reached my location, I would leap to my death.

The unobstructed moonlight atop that cliff shined brighter than down below. I never will forget that. It seemed a little too bright. Suddenly, out of nowhere, a cold rain came. The wet didn't really bother me except for the water that ran down from my head into my face. I wiped my face clean of water and when I removed my hands, there was Death staring at me— standing right in front of me! It had to be Death because the figure was too frightening to be anything else. He looked like a skeleton with ragged clothes on, the kind of skeleton you might see on the bottle of poison, only the skull and bones were the color of blood. He didn't say anything; he just looked through me with those big, hollow black eye sockets. My body went stiff from fright. I moved backward and away, my eyes fixed on him, my hands up as if ready to grapple. He didn't follow; just watched me. That's when the train screeched past underneath us, a shot of upward draft blasting me back to my senses. I didn't wait for the long train to fully pass. As soon as I found a safe way down, I hurried to the ground, looking up and back as I ran parallel but counter to the train, searching the cliff to see if Death was still there. He was, and he was still watching me. Once the train passed, I crossed the tracks back to the highway. I slowed my pace only after Death was out of sight.

*Thank you, Lord, for showing me how foolish I've been. I'm going home to talk this out with my wife.* I was convinced that the whole thing was God scaring me away from suicide so I would return to my wife and children, even if my wife felt she no longer wanted me. Once back home, I began the process of mending my relationship with Essie. When Essie became pregnant with our sixth child, Angela, Essie agreed to move with me to a house we bought across the street from the church in Littlerock. It was a modest house, but Essie did a wonderful job making it a home. It didn't take long, however, for me to see that desert living was not suitable to Essie's sensibilities, just like she'd been saying for years. We decided to move to Lancaster, a medium-sized city just 20 miles from my church and 30 miles from my job at Edwards AFB.

Sadly, we would divorce just a few years later. Of course, the divorce broke my heart, but I did not let it devastate me. That cliff-top experience, where I literally faced Death, had taught me to value the life God gave me, regardless of any hardships or struggles. I had learned that no matter what happened to me or where I went, God was with me, and in that I've found true and lasting peace.

Jesus said in John 16:33 (NIV), *"I have told you these things that in me you may have peace. In this world, you will have trouble! But take heart! I have overcome the world."* In the world, we face troubles. In Christ, we overcome. In the world, we find despair. In Christ, we find *peace*.

CHAPTER SIXTEEN

# THE HEAVENS DECLARE HIS GLORY

## EDWARDS AFB AND TWENTY YEARS OF SERVICE

If you have ever even been close to Edwards Air Force Base (AFB), you've likely found your attention drawn upward by heart-stopping sonic booms, the result of supersonic aircraft piercing the sound barrier. You've likely watched as heroic pilots tease the steel-blue bonds of heaven with advanced fighter jets and stealthy sub-space technology. You may have even had the privilege of being at Edwards AFB on the few occasions when the Space Shuttle landed, and rerouted to Edwards because of inclement weather at Cape Canaveral. Yes, Edwards was and still is a dynamic place, and I loved working there and playing a small part in its historic achievements. Let me list just a few of the monumental milestones reached and exceeded there over the past 60 years:

- On October 1, 1942, America's first jet aircraft, the XP-59, flew for the first time.
- On October 14, 1947, Chuck Yeager, whom I know personally, first broke the sound barrier in the experimental X-1 jet aircraft.

- On July 17, 1962, Bob White became the first man ever to fly an aircraft into space, the X-15, reaching an altitude of 354,200 feet (67 miles).
- On October 3, 1967, William J. "Pete" Knight, whom I have also had the pleasure to know, set an aircraft speed record of Mach 6.72 (hypersonic 4,520 mph), also in the X-15 experimental aircraft—a record that stands to this day.[4]

And the NASA-Dryden Flight Research Center at Edwards AFB played a pivotal role in the development of our nation's space program, to include the building and testing of the Lunar Landing Modules astronauts would pilot to land on the moon and, later, the development and testing of the Space Shuttle.

I list a few of these achievements and their dates so you'll understand why, as I mentioned in the previous chapter, I could not pass on the opportunity to work at Edwards as an engineer. In 1968, when the position opened up, our nation had gotten to within one year of putting the first man on the moon, which happened in July 1969. And though the spacecraft were being launched from Cape Canaveral, Florida, much of the testing of jet propulsion and for manned space flight was being done at Edwards. In fact, many of the astronauts selected for the space program came from the pool of test pilots flying at Edwards, some of whom I've come to know and love. To be able to play even a bit part in that history would be amazing.

I submitted my résumé the same day I saw the job announcement. I was immediately sent by Base Personnel to see Bill Bassett, chief engineer

---

4 Luther, Craig W. *X-Planes at Edwards AFB*. Edwards Air Force Base, California: Air Force Flight Test Center History Office, 2007.

of the Civil Engineering Branch, who interviewed and hired me on the spot. Unbeknownst to me, Bill had heard my keynote speech at the first Dr. Martin Luther King, Jr. memorial service held in the Antelope Valley. Dr. King was assassinated April 4, 1968, just a couple months before my July interview. Bill had taken his adolescent daughter to the MLK memorial service so she could learn more about the historic significance of his assassination and his contribution to American race relations. During the interview, Bill confided in me that he'd been impressed with my speaking ability. To my surprise, after asking me a few questions about my civil engineering background, he asked about Dr. King. It was a sincere inquiry from a man with a genuine concern for what Dr. King's assassination meant for the country. Still, after he finished with his questions, I felt compelled to tell him, "I don't want to be your black engineer, just your best engineer." He smiled at that one.

After orientation, Bill assigned me a desk in what they called "the bullpen," a large open area where all the civil engineers were seated. Civil engineering encompasses several sub-disciplines, including structural engineering. That's where Bill placed me. He wanted me to fill a structural engineer's slot, which had a large emphasis on concrete structures—like runways, aircraft hangers, and just about any other type of building. Later, they tasked me with leading full projects where I got the chance to build jet propulsion buildings, the Integrated Flight Avionics Systems (IFAS) Test Center and the Ridley Mission Control Center, which continues to serve as the heart of the Air Force Flight Test Center, tracking and recording nearly all flight test operations.[5] Those are some of my proudest accomplishments during my 20 years at Edwards AFB.

---

[5] Thuloweit, Kenji, *Ridley Mission Control Center Turns 30*, Edwards Air Force Base, California, 95th Air Base Wing Public Affairs, retrieved May 3, 2013, http://www.edwards.af.mil/ news/story .asp?id=123208535

Another project I was proud of got off to a bumpy start but ended beautifully. It was 1972, and I was tasked with assembling a team of professionals to build a tracking system link that would help track *Skylab* and any subsequent manned earth orbiters, like the Space Shuttle. Skylab, conceived in 1963, was America's first space lab station. Our portion of the tracking system would need to link from Edwards to Vandenberg AFB's tracking link and to another link in Salt Lake City, Utah. My new boss, Charles "Pete" Adolph, who would later become technical director of the Air Force Flight Test Center, brought the planned system drawings and asked me to oversee the entire project. My training was in civil engineering, however, so I understood very little about electrical engineering, avionics, radar systems, transmitters, or the like. Still, Pete put the project squarely on my shoulders, with complete authority to hire anyone I deemed essential to the mission.

During the process of selecting personnel for the project, a gentleman's name came up who was known on the base as an expert in tracking system technology. There was only one problem: he had been overheard saying he would never work for a "nigger." I won't mention his name because I have no grudge to bear, but I decided I wanted him anyway and went to pay him a visit at his office.

He said, "I know why you're here, and I'm not working for a nigger! And even if you weren't a nigger, all the civil engineers I've ever met are nothing but idiots . . . dummies who don't know their behinds from their heads!"

I said, "Well, part of what you said is true. I am a civil engineer, and I sure can be a dummy at times. But I don't quite know what a 'nigger' is, so you'll have to explain that one to me."

He says, "You know what a nigger is because you are one! Now go on! I'm not interested in your project!"

I accepted the fact that I did not know anything about the tracking system. If you change your mind, I sure would be glad for your help. A couple of hours later, he came to my office and said, "What is it that you want and when do we have to start?" I looked at him and said, "We start now. If I don't know something, you can tell me what I need."

At first, he spewed bitterness and verbal abuse my way, but as time went on, his demeanor toward me changed. He became more open and trusting, which led to a lasting friendship over time.

One time, while we were laughing and chatting about something, I saw vulnerability in his eyes that I'd never seen before like he wanted to discuss our past but was afraid. Perhaps he wanted to apologize or simply explain his harsh words. Whatever it was, it remained buried in his heart. I can only hope that my actions toward him let him know I harbored no resentment or grudge. I just did as Jesus would have done. I tried to show grace. And grace, I've learned, triumphs over race every time.

Sometime later, he came to me, not as his boss but as a preacher.

"Hank," he said (that's what they called me), "I need your help. My mother-in-law is sick. From what I've learned about you, I'm convinced that if you prayed over her, she would get well."

His faith in me blew me away! Truthfully, he demonstrated more faith in God than in me, I suppose. I had no power to heal, but I did have the ability to pray that God would heal. Together, we prayed over her, and out of that experience, we developed a close friendship. When he died in 2014, I spoke at his funeral. That's what grace can do.

About halfway through my 20-year stint at Edwards, I transferred from the Civil Engineering Branch to the Environmental Branch, which was responsible for monitoring the environmental impact of any and all base operations. It was a monumental task at a 481-square-mile flight test installation with over 10,000 military and civilian personnel and no fewer than 53 regulatory agencies auditing our assessments and reports. Any company, organization, or person wanting to conduct operations on Edwards had to come through my office. That position also required top-secret Special Background Investigation (SBI) security clearance, permitting me up close and personal access to areas and projects rarely seen by human eyes. I welcomed the responsibility. By the time I retired in 1989, I had become head of the entire branch with nearly 100 employees under me.

In addition to those experiences, the government gave me the opportunity to attend the University of Southern California (USC), where I earned a Master's Degree in Environmental Engineering. I also had the pleasure of meeting many astronauts and heroes of flight while at Edwards, people like Neil Armstrong and Buzz Aldrin, who flew with Michael Collins on Apollo 11 and became the first humans to land on the moon; John Glenn, Joe Walker, Alan Shepherd, Jim Lovell, Tom Stafford. I came to know many of these pilots and astronauts as friends. It might surprise you to know that Armstrong and Aldrin took communion on the moon. Aldrin carried with him a wonderful prayer written by James Dillet Freeman for the troops fighting in WWII. First published in 1941, Freeman's *Prayer For Protection* is known the world over and is a staple of many Christmas Eve services.[6]

My time at Edwards brought me tremendous satisfaction and joy. Sadly, the increased responsibility that came with it would negatively impact other areas of my life, including my pastorship at First Missionary Baptist Church.

Writing this chapter reminded me that our lives are not one-dimensional but rather multifaceted. We are spouses, parents, colleagues, parishioners, siblings, children, students, volunteers, evangelists,

---

6 James Dillet Freeman, *Prayer For Protection*, Unity Magazine, Unity.org, retrieved May 4, 2013, http://www.unity.org/resources/articles/prayer-protection

missionaries and many other things. We must remain cognizant of not only our priorities but also what we are sacrificing by prioritizing one area over another. It is impossible to be in two places at one time, even in an ever-increasing virtual world. If we pray for guidance from our Heavenly Father, we will prioritize our lives according to His good and perfect will, not our own.

CHAPTER SEVENTEEN

# THE DEATH OF HOPE—1968

**LADIES AND GENTLEMEN,**

"I'm only going to talk to you just for a minute or so this evening because I have some—some very sad news for all of you—

Could you lower those signs, please?—I have some very sad news for all of you, and, I think, sad news for all of our fellow citizens and people who love peace all over the world; and that is that Martin Luther King was shot and was killed tonight in Memphis, Tennessee.

> *"Martin Luther King dedicated his life to love and to justice between fellow human beings. He died in the cause of that effort. In this difficult day, in this difficult time for the United States, it's perhaps well to ask what kind of a nation we are and what direction we want to move in. For those of you who are black—considering the evidence evidently is that there were white people who were responsible—you can be filled with bitterness, and with hatred, and a desire for revenge.*
>
> *"We can move in that direction as a country, in greater polarization—black people amongst blacks, and white amongst whites, filled with hatred toward one another. Or we can make an effort, as Martin Luther King did, to*

*understand, and to comprehend, and replace that violence, that stain of bloodshed that has spread across our land, with an effort to understand, compassion, and love.*

*"For those of you who are black and are tempted to fill with—be filled with hatred and mistrust of the injustice of such an act against all white people, I would only say that I can also feel in my own heart the same kind of feeling. I had a member of my family killed, but he was killed by a white man.*

*"But we have to make an effort in the United States. We have to make an effort to understand, to get beyond, or go beyond these rather difficult times.*

*"My favorite poem, my—my favorite poet was Aeschylus. And he once wrote:*

*'Even in our sleep, pain which cannot forget falls drop by drop upon the heart, until, in our own despair, against our will, comes wisdom through the awful grace of God.'*

*"What we need in the United States is not division; what we need in the United States is not hatred; what we need in the United States is not violence and lawlessness, but is love, and wisdom, and compassion toward one another, and a feeling of justice toward those who still suffer within our country, whether they be white or whether they be black.*

*"So I ask you tonight to return home, to say a prayer for the family of Martin Luther King—yeah, it's true—but more importantly to say a prayer for our own country, which all of us love—a prayer for understanding and that compassion of which I spoke.*

*"We can do well in this country. We will have difficult times. We've had difficult times in the past, but we—and we*

## The Death of Hope—1968

*will have difficult times in the future. It is not the end of violence; it is not the end of lawlessness, and it's not the end of disorder.*

*"But the vast majority of white people and the vast majority of black people in this country want to live together, want to improve the quality of our life and want justice for all human beings that abide in our land.*

*"And let's dedicate ourselves to what the Greeks wrote so many years ago: to tame the savageness of man and make gentle the life of this world. Let us dedicate ourselves to that and say a prayer for our country and for our people.*

*"Thank you very much."*[7]

Robert F. Kennedy delivered those poetic yet impromptu comments in Indianapolis, Indiana, on the night of April 4, 1968, just hours after Dr. King's assassination.

Dr. King was standing on the balcony of the Lorraine Motel in Memphis, Tennessee, not far from TSU, where I had attended college. He was just outside of room 306 when, at 6:01p.m. Thursday, April 4, 1968, James Earl Ray fired his .30 caliber rifle from a building across the street, the bullet striking Dr. King in the neck, severing a jugular vein. He survived the shooting but was pronounced dead by doctors at St. Joseph's Hospital an hour later.

I was still working in San Fernando and preaching in Littlerock at that time and had just arrived home from the office. Tennessee is a couple hours ahead of California. The news would have been hitting the California airwaves around four or five in the evening. Essie called me at

---

7 Kennedy, Robert F. *"Remarks on the Assassination of Martin Luther King, Jr."* (Speech, Indianapolis, IN, 1968-04-04), American Rhetoric Online Speech Bank. Retrieved May. 4, 2013

work with the terrible news, and I rushed home to find her sitting on the couch watching the television news, crying as the kids huddled close. We must have watched the coverage all night long, and I know that neither of us got much sleep that night.

The reason I chose to lead this chapter with comments by Robert F. Kennedy rather than a quote from Dr. King is that Kennedy's words seem to best capture what my heart felt back in 1968, the moment I heard Martin—the face of Civil Rights and a hero to so many, including myself—had been assassinated. My solemn prayer immediately was that our nation would not move, as Kennedy so emotionally put it, toward further divisiveness, bitterness, and hatred, or destructive violence but rather in the direction of greater understanding, compassion, and love between people, no matter their race, religion, or political party. To become bitter and violent, I concluded, to hate one another more as a result of Dr. King's death would have gone against what he stood for and would have risked negating much of the progress he and other peaceful activists made toward equality and the understanding that we are all God's beloved children. He warned us of such in a seldom-quoted excerpt from his most famous speech, *I Have A Dream:*

> *"But there is something that I must say to my people, who stand on the warm threshold which leads into the palace of justice: In the process of gaining our rightful place, we must not be guilty of wrongful deeds. Let us not seek to satisfy our thirst for freedom by drinking from the cup of bitterness and hatred. We must forever conduct our struggle on the high plane of dignity and discipline. We must not allow our creative protest to degenerate into physical violence. Again and again, we must rise to the majestic heights of meeting physical force with soul force.*

## The Death of Hope—1968

> "The marvelous new militancy which has engulfed the Negro community must not lead us to a distrust of all white people, for many of our white brothers, as evidenced by their presence here today, have come to realize that their destiny is tied up with our destiny. And they have come to realize that their freedom is inextricably bound to our freedom. We cannot walk alone. And as we walk, we must make the pledge that we shall always march ahead. We cannot turn back."[8]

I suppose my prayer came from a profound sense of emptiness upon learning of Martin's death—like *hope* had been assassinated. What I was doing in my little neighborhood for race relations could never compare to what Dr. King had done for the nation. I thought: *What in the world will we do now that this great man is gone?*

There were others in his entourage who could pick up Dr. King's mantle of civil rights, but to me, they were not as unifying as Martin. They seemed to have other agendas that didn't suit fully with me.

John F. Kennedy was another voice for civil rights who had been assassinated. I wondered who would be next. Of course, just two short months later, we saw Robert F. Kennedy assassinated as well. Those three assassinations reminded me that our nation was in desperate need of a healing savior. If history has shown us anything, it's that no mortal man has ever been capable of healing our land. And no man—not John F. Kennedy, not Robert F. Kennedy, not even Martin Luther King, Jr.—could ever fill the role of Savior. For healing and saving, we would need to once again turn to the God, who has blessed this country from the

---

8 Dr. Martin Luther King, Jr., *I Have A Dream* Speech, Delivered August 28, 1963 at the Washington Memorial, Washington DC, American Rhetoric Top 100 Speeches, Retrieved May 4, 2013, http://www.americanrhetoric.com/speeches/mlkihaveadream.htm

beginning. Remember God's admonition to the Jews in 2 Chronicles 7:14 (NIV): *"If my people, who are called by my name, will humble themselves and pray and seek my face and turn from their wicked ways, then I will hear from heaven, and I will forgive their sin and will heal their land."*

When we come to Christ as individuals, He receives us with open arms and unconditional love. Those are His gifts to us, which He wants us to pass on to others in His name. But in order to come to Christ, we must first acknowledge that *He is*—that He exists and is who He claims to be. It's not a condition, just a fact. Think about it this way: How could I ever accept gifts from you, especially your love, if I deny you even exist? The same applies to nations. This nation was founded on Christian principles, but with time, we have strayed, denying God more and more. The more we deny Him, the less we love each other in His name. To me, that is what the above verse is all about. God seems to be saying, "Remember me? Remember how much I love you? Please don't forget that love I have for you. When you remember how much I, the God of all, love you, then you will love each other more, and the healing can begin."

Sadly, violence would erupt after Martin's killing, at least for a time, signaling the healing would have to wait. Riots sparked in just about every major city in the United States. When the anger subsided, 35 people had been killed, thousands had been injured, and blocks upon blocks of major cities had been burned. Los Angeles, of which San Fernando and Pacoima were linked, was no exception. I felt a deep ache in my soul, perhaps even more in the days following Martin's assassination, as I watched television coverage with my wife and young children of the riots across the nation and as I heard the death toll and injury count rise.

Most of the civil rights leaders of that time came out and called for calm, but not all. Here are just two contrasting statements put out by black leaders immediately following Martin's assassination. They illustrate the understandably turbulent sentiment swirling after his tragic and senseless killing. Activist Stokely Carmichael perhaps incited the worst response when he proclaimed:

> *"White America killed Dr. King last night. She made [it] a whole lot easier for a whole lot of black people today. There no longer needs to be intellectual discussions. Black people know that they have to get guns. White America will live to cry that she killed Dr. King last night. It would have been better if she had killed Rap Brown and/or Stokley Carmichael, but when she killed Dr. King, she lost."* [9]

James Farmer, Jr., who later held the position of assistant secretary of what is now known as Health and Human Services (under Republican President Richard Nixon), countered, urging restraint and peaceful protest:

> *"Dr. King would be greatly distressed to find that his blood had triggered off bloodshed and disorder, that is—when it is accounted to his entire life. I think instead, the nation should be quiet, black and white, and we should be in a prayerful mood, which would be in keeping with his life. We should make that kind of dedication and commitment to the goals which his life served to solving the domestic problems. That's the memorial. That's the kind of memorial we should build for him. It's just not appropriate for there to be violent retaliations and that kind of demonstration in the wake of the murder of this pacifist and man of peace."* [10]

---

9 Martin Luther King Assassination (transcript), *Events of 1968—Year In Review*, United Press International, Inc., UPI.com, Retrieved May 6, 2013, http://www.upi.com/Audio/Year_in_Review/Events-of-1968/Martin-Luther-King-Assasination/12303153093431-4/
10 Martin Luther King Assassination (transcript), *Events of 1968—Year In Review*, United Press International, Inc., UPI.com, Retrieved May 6, 2013, http://www.upi.com/Audio/Year_in_Review/Events-of-1968/Martin-Luther-King-Assasination/12303153093431-4/

But perhaps nobody said it better than King himself when asked by a journalist how he would like to be remembered:

> *If any of you [are] around when I have to meet my day, I don't want a long funeral. And if you get somebody to deliver the eulogy, tell him not to talk too long. Every now and then, I wonder what I want him to say. Tell him not to mention that I have a Nobel Peace Prize. That isn't important. Tell him not to mention that I have 300 or 400 other awards; that's not important. Tell him not to mention where I went to school.*
>
> *"I'd like somebody to mention that day that Martin Luther King, Jr. tried to give his life serving others. I'd like for somebody to say that day that Martin Luther King Jr. tried to love somebody. I want you to say that day that I've tried to be right on the walk with them. I want you to be able to say that day that I did try to feed the hungry. I want you to be able to say that day that I did try in my life to clothe all the naked. I want you to say on that day that I did try in my life to visit those who were in prison. And I want you to say that I tried to love and serve humanity.*
>
> *"Yes, if you want to say that I was a drum major, say that I was a drum major for justice. Say that I was a drum major for peace. I was a drum major for righteousness. And all of the other shallow things will not matter."*[11]

---

11 Martin Luther King Assassination (transcript), *Events of 1968—Year In Review*, United Press International, Inc., UPI.com, Retrieved May 6, 2013, http://www.upi.com/Audio/Year_in_Review/Events-of-1968/Martin-Luther-King-Assasination/12303153093431-4/

## The Death of Hope—1968

So what is the point in my revealing and recapping all of this history, supporting it with so many quotes and speeches? The reason is this: time has a way of neutralizing the emotional impact of critical events, dooming us to let our guard down and repeat them. We must remember—not to hold onto the past, but to remind us of how far we've come so we won't go backward. Dr. King stood for greater unity, not greater separation; more love between people, not more discord; harmony and peace, not conflict and violence. We must remember this. And we must remember that if we want others to love us, we must also love them, even through the mistakes. If we don't, then lasting unity, lasting harmony and peace, and even lasting love are all impossible. It takes at least two people to achieve each.

Just two days after Dr. King was killed, with the help of others, I organized a tribute service at the Methodist church in Lancaster, California. It was a wonderful, peaceful, solemn, interracial gathering. People spoke and gave testimonies, and I gave the keynote address. I believe our tribute was one of the first in the nation, with local media present to witness the healing process begin.

Another thing I did was to have my good friend, Pastor E.V. Hill, speak at my church. Hill, one of the most-respected conservative clergymen of the twentieth century, was also a civil-rights icon and close confidant of Dr. King and the Rev. Billy Graham. He served as pastor of Mt. Zion Missionary Baptist Church, a house of worship located in the heart of Watts, where some of the riots occurred following Dr. King's assassination. We invited the surrounding community to hear E.V. speak as well, filling our small church to capacity. He laid down some beautiful words. He shared how Dr. King had followed Jesus to the cross, giving his life just as Jesus had in the name of love, justice, and peace. He talked about how both had opened the eyes of the world through grace, not hate. Sadly, E.V. died in 2003, but his memory, like Dr. King's, lives on.

Every year since our first tribute, we've had prominent voices speak at our annual MLK gatherings. Our speakers have included Coretta Scott King, Dr. King's wife, his children on another occasion, and Alex Haley, author of Roots (seen shaking my hand in the photo below).

Time would eventually bring about the change Martin sought for this beloved country. For me personally, that change solidified itself with my election to the Lancaster City Council and as the first African American appointed mayor of the same city. Once in office, I pushed to make Dr. King's birthday a city holiday (at that time, the federal government had left it up to local and state governments). Ultimately, with the help of a delegation of interracial and interdenominational pastors from our community, I was able to petition the City Council for a local Dr. Martin Luther King Jr. holiday. They voted unanimously five to zero in favor, leading many nearby cities to follow suit, culminating in the now nationally-recognized holiday.

In the aftermath of Dr. King's assassination, my own church, a predominantly black congregation at that time, was not immune to confusion and discord. I remember in 1969, just a year after Dr. King's death, the deacons of my church urging me to take a larger role in civil rights, but with all of my professional and familial responsibilities, it just wasn't to be. I did what I could, of course, but the deacons were dissatisfied. Like I mentioned earlier, confusion reigned for a time after Dr. King's assassination, particularly in the black community of this nation. No was not a very popular word back then for blacks. Unfortunately, that's how some of the deacons of my church took my inability to carry the torch of civil rights, and while away on training for my new job at Edwards, the disgruntled deacons organized a coup.

Not all were onboard with their scheme, however. One deacon called me in Ohio to let me know what had happened. I said to the man who called, "Brother Thomas, do not worry about this. God sees what is happening and will take care of it."

Within about two hours of that conversation, I received another call telling me that the deacon who had led the revolt died from sudden cardiac arrest—a heart attack. Perhaps it was a coincidence, perhaps not, but it shook the deacon board, most of whom were elderly. Still, when I returned from my trip, I found that the locks to First Missionary Baptist Church had been changed, and I had been removed from my role as pastor.

Never one to step aside so easily, I asked to be let into my office to retrieve my things. Once inside, I resumed my rightful place behind my desk, refusing to leave until we had an honest vote, not one done in secret while I was away, but one in the presence of the entire congregation. I knew that most wanted me to stay but had felt no say in the matter.

I called a meeting of the entire church body, including the deacons and a notary public. I asked for the deacons to explain the problem they had with me. They said that I didn't do things the way a normal black preacher did things. What they meant is that I was not an outspoken critic of white injustice. They wanted me active, not passive. But my way of effecting change was with love and grace, not confrontation.

I called for another vote to keep or remove me as pastor, this time by the entire church body and to be formally recorded by the notary. The 70 or so members voted unanimously for me to stay. In addition, they asked that the deacon board formally apologize to me. Some refused, however, and were voted out by the body, their positions to be filled by others.

Those deacons refusing to apologize left the church for good that evening, but wouldn't you know that another of them died just a month or two after the vote, and then another died a month later! Now, I started feeling anxious because I had handled their disruption swiftly and somewhat forcefully. Now those people were dying! Again, these were all older gentlemen, making it perhaps more coincidence than divine judgment. Still, I started thinking, *Wow! I sure hope I don't mess this up, or else I may be next!*

Not long after that third former deacon died, I received an urgent phone call from a fourth, Deacon Battle, who was frail and in his 90s. He pleaded for me to come see him. When I arrived at his home, he said to me, "Pastor . . . I think I was supposed to die last night, but I asked the Lord for a little more time so I could ask your forgiveness. God showed me that I was wrong about you, and I want to apologize. Will you please forgive me, Pastor?"

I said warmly, "Absolutely. Will you forgive me for being so harsh about everything upon my return from Ohio . . . for disrespecting an elder like you in the church?"

He said, "Of course, but son, will you please forgive me so I can go home to be with our Lord?"

It was so touching. Of course, I forgave him. How could I not? Jesus had forgiven me from the cross and for so much worse! Before I left his home, he confessed that the Lord had revealed to him that First Missionary

Baptist Church would grow under my leadership, acquire many more acres and buildings, and have hundreds more attending of every race and ethnicity. Then he said, "Don't let anybody like me run you off. Do not leave the church."

He was in a rocking chair, and I knelt to hug him. He asked if I would help him to bed, so I picked him up and carried his frail body to his bed, gently laid him down, and then, as I tucked him in, asked if he was comfortable. But he was already gone, peace on his face, forever home with the Lord.

I'll close this chapter with those famous words from Dr. King's speech, *I Have A Dream*:

> *"Let us not wallow in the valley of despair, I say to you today, my friends. And so, even though we face the difficulties of today and tomorrow, I still have a dream. It is a dream deeply rooted in the American dream. I have a dream that one day, this nation will rise up and live out the true meaning of its creed: 'We hold these truths to be self-evident, that all men are created equal.' I have a dream that one day, on the red hills of Georgia, the sons of former slaves and the sons of former slave owners will be able to sit down together at the table of brotherhood. I have a dream that one day, even the state of Mississippi, a state sweltering with the heat of injustice, sweltering with the heat of oppression, will be transformed into an oasis of freedom and justice.*

"I have a dream that my four little children will one day live in a nation where they will not be judged by the color of their skin but by the content of their character. I have a dream today! I have a dream that one day, down in Alabama . . . little black boys and black girls will be able to join hands with little white boys and white girls as sisters and brothers. I have a dream today! I have a dream that one day every valley shall be exalted, and every hill and mountain shall be made low, the rough places will be made plain, and the crooked places will be made straight; 'and the glory of the Lord shall be revealed, and all flesh shall see it together.'"[12]

---

[12] Dr. Martin Luther King, Jr., *I Have A Dream* Speech, Delivered August 28, 1963 at the Washington Memorial, Washington DC, American Rhetoric Top 100 Speeches, Retrieved May 4, 2013, http://www.americanrhetoric.com/speeches/mlkihaveadream.htm

CHAPTER EIGHTEEN

# FAITH, PARTY, AND POLITICS—EIGHTEEN YEARS OF PUBLIC SERVICE

What made me get into politics? In 1989, I was 56 years old, about to retire from my career at Edwards AFB and living across the street from Jan Spencer, senior pastor of the Living Way Foursquare Church in Lancaster. One morning Jan came to me and said, "Henry, I'm talking to you about something I know God is not calling me to do, but which is still of importance to this community. We need a godly man to run our city."

I said, "Jan, if you're implying that I should run for political office, I'm not interested. I pastor a church just like you and I'm happy doing that."

Later that same day, another friend said something very similar to me that the City was in terrible shape and needed a godly man like me to straighten it out. Were the two conversations a coincidence? Perhaps. But maybe God really was calling me into politics.

Over the next week or so, I prayed for God to reveal Himself in that decision, waiting with blessed assurance that he would answer one way or the other. Shortly thereafter came the week of my retirement from Edwards AFB, which wasn't far from Lancaster, California—maybe 30 miles. In fact, most of the civil servants working at Edwards, including my boss, lived in Lancaster or Palmdale (an adjoining city). While cleaning out my office, my boss came in and asked what my post-retirement plans entailed, reminding me that I had plenty of good years ahead of me. I mentioned spending more time growing the church and such, and spending time with my wonderful children. That's when he said to me, "Henry, why don't you see if you can get Lancaster back on track? Just might be that you're the man for the job."

I knew then that God was calling me to run for political office. Three people in less than two weeks telling me I should run was much more than coincidence, so I threw my hat into the political lion cage, running for a seat on the Lancaster City Council. I pulled papers, and the rest is history. Jan and many others helped on my campaign, and in 1990, the citizens of Lancaster elected me as one of their trusted council members— the first African American ever elected to that council. At that time the mayor position was not elected, but rather chosen by the council from sitting council members. In 1991, the other council members chose me as the first African-American mayor of Lancaster.

That first year presented a few challenges for me as a preacher-politician, one of which was the issuing or denying of business licenses to businesses wanting to operate within city limits. Of particular issue for me were the liquor stores and pornography businesses. As a preacher, I recognized the problems these two types of businesses brought with them to any city. Churches are filled with hurting souls, people who have destroyed valuable marriages, relationships with family and friends, and their own lives by addictions to both alcohol and pornography. Yes, there would be tax dollars for the city, but also moral decay, alcohol-related violence, and a host of other issues. My vote was always no. Unfortunately,

I quickly learned that entrepreneurs have the right to operate a certain number of these businesses within city limits.

I did what I could to limit the number allowed, leading one of the strongest fights against pornography ever seen in our community. In my mind, the Bible, God's word, says certain things are wrong, and you just don't do them. You certainly don't vote to allow them a foothold or to validate them in any way, not if you are trying to build up God's kingdom.

With that in mind, it didn't take long before the cries of "separation of church and state" echoed from the city's depths. Even something as simple as how I wanted my name listed became a big controversy. I'll get to that in a moment, but before I do, I think it's important to understand where the mantra of "separation of church and state" came from so both present and future generations have a leg to stand on in this argument.

This phrase, "separation of church and state," has become the battle cry of atheist groups across this nation bent on one thing: eradicating the free expression of religion, particularly Christianity, in any publicly-funded square or by any public servant utilizing the bully pulpit of office. The phrase was taken from a letter written by Thomas Jefferson to the Danbury Baptists of Connecticut in 1802, the transcript can be obtained from the Library of Congress:

> *"Believing with you that religion is a matter which lies solely between Man & his God, that he owes account to none other for his faith or his worship, that the legitimate powers of government reach actions only, & not opinions, I contemplate with sovereign reverence that act of the whole American people which declared that their legislature should "make no law respecting an establishment of religion, or prohibiting the free exercise thereof," thus building a wall of separation between Church & State. Adhering to this expression of the*

*supreme will of the nation in behalf of the rights of conscience, I shall see with sincere satisfaction the progress of those sentiments which tend to restore to man all his natural rights, convinced he has no natural right in opposition to his social duties.*

*"I reciprocate your kind prayers for the protection & blessing of the common father and creator of man, and tender you for yourselves & your religious association, assurances of my high respect & esteem," Jefferson wrote.*[13]

It has been, and continues to be, this letter atheist groups cite out of context to silence public officials caught proclaiming the name of Christ (I say Christ because I have yet to hear of any other religion being stripped from the lips of public servants), knowing full well that most of us will never research the true intent of this letter, nor the faith of the man who penned it. Jefferson was a man of strong Christian conviction, and the purpose of the letter was to assuage the concerns of the Danbury Baptists that the United States government intended to restrict their religious freedom. Jefferson wrote this letter to affirm his own faith and to reaffirm the nation's commitment to the U. S. Constitution, namely the First Amendment, which Jefferson quotes in the letter. *"Congress shall make no law respecting an establishment of religion, or prohibiting the free exercise thereof, or abridging the freedom of speech, or of the press; or the right of the people peaceably to assemble, and to petition the Government for a redress of grievances."*[14]

---

13 Thomas Jefferson, *Jefferson's Letter to the Danbury Baptists*, 1802, Library of Congress, Retrieved May 13, 2013, http://www.loc.gov/loc/lcib/9806/danpre.html
14 First Amendment, Ratified December 15, 1791, Constitution of the United States

*Faith, Party, and Politics—Eighteen Years of Public Service*

The Danbury Baptists thought the government intended to establish another denomination, which in those days was synonymous with the word religion, as the national religion. Jefferson proclaimed that a "wall of separation between church and state" existed to protect the "free exercise" of their faith, not to say that politicians are prohibited from aligning themselves with any particular religion, nor to say that politicians were exempted from "the free exercise thereof." Public servants are bound by the Constitution and swear to uphold it when they take office. They do not forego the rights granted them under the Constitution when they become public servants. That is what atheist groups want us to believe, and it is an unabated lie.

It's also important to understand why the First Amendment to the United States Constitution was enacted. The Puritans of England were being persecuted by the British government, which had just aligned itself with the Anglican Church, making Anglican the only recognized church or religion of England. Many Puritans fled to *The New World*, the Americas, so they could be *free to exercise* their faith without fear of persecution.

Now, with that history fresh in your mind, let me talk about a few of the struggles I faced as a preacher-politician. The first had to do with my name and title. I wanted my title, Reverend, to appear before my name on all public nomenclature, whether business cards, letterhead, nameplates, or my signature. I felt it was important that everybody understand I was and would remain the same person they had elected—a follower of Jesus first, a preacher and family man second, and a politician third. Still, those who were against me said "Reverend" could not precede my name while serving in political office. People knew me as Reverend Hearns so that news upset me.

Well, after doing some due diligence, I found that a title defining a politician's training and profession, such as Doctor, was allowed, so why not Reverend? I was an ordained minister of the gospel, a title recognized legally in any court of law. In the end, my team won that legal challenge. From that moment on, people called me Councilman Reverend Hearns or Mayor Reverend Hearns. Some even referred to me as Reverend Mayor, an endearing title I kind of liked.

Another controversial thing I did was to lead a prayer at council meetings. Of course, the American Civil Liberties Union (ACLU), which is arguably and ironically given their organization's name, the strongest opposition to public proclamations of faith, particularly Christianity, fired off a letter telling me to cease and desist praying at council meetings or face a lawsuit. I responded kindly, stating I would give their order careful consideration, and I just kept considering that for 18 more years, having never ceased or desisted in public prayer as mayor, honorary mayor, or council member. Jesus told us in Matthew 10:16 (NIV), *"I am sending you out like sheep among wolves. Therefore, be as shrewd as snakes and as innocent as doves."*

The ACLU filed the lawsuit as promised. The Ninth Circuit Court of Appeals in 2013 supported my position. It upheld the right to public prayer because the selection process was changed in 2009 for a citizen panel to select speakers from all religions, and specifically, my invoking the name of Jesus during prayers before city council meetings did not endorse Christianity for the city.[15]

I got a lot of pushback from other religious groups in the area, too, particularly the Muslim and Jewish communities, for espousing my Christian beliefs from the bully pulpit. Once while serving as mayor, members from the Jewish community called for a meeting with me at one of the Jewish synagogues in town. There were about 200 people there, and they went after me right from the start, telling me that I was

---

15 Hull, Tim, Courthouse News Service, CA "City Council Prayers Didn't Endorse Jesus." March 26, 2013, http://www.courthousenews.com/2013/03/26/56068.htm Retrieved April, 3 2015

## Faith, Party, and Politics—Eighteen Years of Public Service

everybody's mayor and not just the mayor for Christians. I understood their concern and listened intently. After all their grievances had been aired, it was my turn to address the crowd. I said, "How many of you heard my campaign speech where I told everybody that I was and will always remain a preacher of the gospel of Jesus Christ?"

About half raised their hands.

I then said, "Now, do you want me to go back on that promise and become a liar? Being a Christian is who I am. It does not mean I support one group over another. *I am* a Christian. It defines me as a man. It does not mean that I am against Muslims, Jews, Hindus, or any other religious group or any other ethnicity. I cannot be anything other than what I am."

Fortunately, there was local realtor with 30 to 40 employees who stood and proclaimed me to be an honest man, telling everybody there that he would help my campaign if I chose to run again. He gave me his business card and told me he would use his phones to help reelect me because honesty in public office was more important to him than religious belief or heritage. In the end, most came out to support me. I also became wonderful friends with the rabbi, a relationship I cherish to this day. I've even spoken at some of their Jewish holiday celebrations.

Sadly, I also received death threats while in office, mostly because I was black. One guy called me directly and said, "You need to know that you're a dead man. We aren't having a nigger running our city."

I said, "Thank you, sir, for your call. I want you to know that I love you as Christ and hope He will bless your life as he has blessed mine."

I caught it from some in the black community, too. Many called me an "Uncle Tom," a derogatory term used amongst African Americans that implies a betrayal of black heritage and unity. The term originates from a time when there were "house niggers" and "field niggers." Most wanted to work in the house where it was warm or cool and where the food was better, as opposed to working the field, which was often more oppressive.

That led some slaves or workers to tell lies about others in hopes that one might be fired and the other moved into the house for being loyal. To some in the black community, I had betrayed my race and heritage. To those few, I was just doing government work to get into the "house" where the getting's good.

You learn quickly in public service that everybody, whether black, white, Hispanic, Christian, Jew, Muslim, or whatever, has a preconceived idea of what values a politician should hold to or what agenda they should push. For me, the best I could do was to be true to Christ and let the rest work itself out. If some thought I was a nigger, so be it; an Uncle Tom, no problem; anti-this or anti-that, okay. But God knew the truth about my motives, and that's all I cared about. As long as I didn't betray Him or my family, then the critics could say and think what they wanted. They just didn't know me.

One fellow preacher in the Antelope Valley, of which Lancaster is a part, invited me to his church on an Easter Sunday before the election in 1990. As I sat there, the preacher proceeded to say, "Rev. Hearns has no business being a politician. All politicians are dogs."

Things got tense all of a sudden, all eyes on me to see how I would respond. I simply smiled, then said playfully, "Bow-wow!"

The congregation laughed so hard that it took several minutes for the preacher who had insulted me to get his house in order again. You just can't worry about what others think about you, not if you want to *serve*.

Other than those few instances, though, serving the public has been a blessing and honor. Most of the citizenry have been very kind and supportive. I've tried to be kind and supportive of them. I've made mistakes, though, as have all politicians.

I once voted for what we called an "evergreen contract" to be given to Waste Management, one of the largest waste collection companies in the world. An evergreen contract meant that it could not be rescinded except

## Faith, Party, and Politics—Eighteen Years of Public Service

for violation of the terms of the contract. That meant the contract was there for life as long as they lived up to their end of the bargain. The contract passed and was awarded, but I soon came to regret that vote when I realized how much the people were against giving anybody that type of contract. I began to pray about it, asking God to provide a way to cancel the evergreen portion of the contract. Not long after, the negotiators for Waste Management asked to modify one area of their contract. In order to do that, the evergreen contract would have to be canceled, and the voting process would need to begin anew. Fortunately, I had a chance to change my vote, as did others, and the evergreen portion of the contract was not re-approved. God had provided! I apologized to the community for the error in judgment, and we moved on.

One of my proudest accomplishments was making it easier for new churches to build in our community; another was the downtown restoration and boulevard improvement, making that area more communal and village-like. I also helped establish the annual Mayor's Prayer Breakfast, which is still a great event. Every year, we have about 700 or 800 hundred people attend. And I helped put in place one of the strongest anti-pornography ordinances in the country. But what I enjoyed most was helping to shape the growth of the city to make it profitable yet safe and a wonderful place to live. I always kept in my mind, "What can I do right now to make life better for just one person?" As time passes, those "one persons" collectively become a lot of people. While I was mayor, we received recognition as "The most business-friendly city in all of Los Angeles County."

I've had the opportunity to meet some great people in America through politics, from everyday citizens who touched my heart to pastors, politicians, and celebrities. I remember meeting Alex Haley, author of the book and television series *Roots* when we invited him to speak at a city event. What a wonderful man! I've had the pleasure of meeting Dr. Martin

Luther King, Jr.'s children and the beloved Rosa Parks. Pastor Jack Hayford who has become a mentor and brother to me. Pastor Tony Evans, another wonderful friend, Pastor Chris Johnson, whom I love as if he were my own son, former Los Angeles Mayor Tom Bradley, Congressman Buck McKeon, Los Angeles 5th District County Supervisor Mike Antonovich, later elected as L.A. mayor, and so many more. God has truly blessed me with the fellowship of inspiring people from all walks of life.

I remember getting to know Tom Bradley before he ever became Los Angeles mayor. I had heard him speak somewhere in San Fernando Valley when he sat on the Los Angeles City Council. We talked afterward and became friends. When I became mayor, he had already served a few years. He invited me down and gave me insights into handling my new mayorship, tips on being a good leader, and so on. Later, when my youngest daughter Angela went off to college, she did a film on Bradley. He reminded me a lot of Dr. King, a soft-spoken man, humbled by his responsibilities and wise beyond measure.

I've met and befriended many of the Space Shuttle astronauts and test pilots, as I mentioned previously. In 1990, the assistant city manager, as a way to boost the city's image, began hosting an annual Wall of Honor, recognizing the achievements of Edward Air Force Base test pilots and the Antelope Valley's heritage in aviation.

People would come in droves. The organizers would ask me to pray at dinner, and there was a space on Sunday morning where we would have breakfast and then get back together from 1 to 2 p.m. Several of the guys would come to service with me.

If I could sum up my experience as a politician and servant of our Lord and His people into one lesson, it would be this: Remember that no matter the cost, stand for your convictions. There will always be detractors and critics, but in the end, you have to answer first to God and second to your conscience.

CHAPTER NINETEEN

# MY DEAREST ESSIE

Essie owned my heart from the first day I saw her to the last—the day she closed her eyes for the final time and went to be with Jesus. Sadly, our marriage did not survive for the duration, but my love and respect for Essie surely did.

I remember when we bought our first house just a couple years after moving to Pacoima, California. We were so happy! We had come from a place and era that oppressed black people, but now we were homeowners. I still recall the address—13239 Eustace Street. The house was a fixer-upper, but we set out to restore it, making it our first real family home. I studied up on sanding and refinishing hardwood flooring and did a nice job rejuvenating that old floor. We painted, fixed the electrical and plumbing issues, did up the yard, and when we were finished, our home was beautiful. It looked brand new! It really had a positive impact on our marriage for a time, too.

Essie was a wonderful mother—a real natural! I think that's one of the things I loved about her most. Our beautiful children are who they are largely because of Essie's love and dedication.

She only stood about 5'6" tall, but she had a dignified presence about her. Essie possessed a delightful stubborn streak. She sure could hold her ground once she made up her mind about something!

Another endearing trait of Essie's was her love for the Lord Jesus, which she enjoyed passing on to the youth at our church by teaching Sunday school and helping to run the Youth Department. In fact, teaching came as natural to Essie as did motherhood.

Essie waited to begin her teaching career until Angela, our youngest child, started kindergarten. But once Essie started teaching, she gave it her whole heart, teaching elementary school in the Antelope Valley for 37 years. Even now, while out and about town, I'll bump into her former students who testify to the impact Essie had on their lives. All of them say the same thing—that Essie was one of their favorite teachers, instructing them not only in their studies but also about life outside of school. And there could have been no better person to teach them life skills than Essie. She placed great value on appearance and on living a moral life, recognizing that both affect how others view us.

When Essie decided on divorce, I was devastated, even despondent for a time. The hurt that overwhelmed my heart cannot be overstated. Like many who endure divorce, my pain manifested itself in some regrettable words toward the woman I had loved since childhood. Those bitter words scarred Essie, causing her to despise me, or so I had thought. What I discovered later, however, just a couple years before Essie went to be with our Lord, was that she had long put those things behind her, just as I had put the pain caused by her leaving behind me.

I believe the year was 2007 when we had our big family reunion in Memphis, Tennessee. It wouldn't have been the same without Essie, so I asked her to come along. Essie was 72 at the time and required a wheelchair on most days. Her body was weakened by cancer and a decade of kidney dialysis. When we arrived at the reunion, I went around to help Essie into the wheelchair. Once seated, she took my left hand, kissed it, and then began to weep.

"Henry, you know God loves me?" Essie said.

"I know He does," I answered. "He surely does."

"Yes," she added, "But he loves me more than most. He must because He gave me the best man He had."

I said, "Ah, Essie, I'm not worth all of that." She nodded, "Yes, you are."

I said, "No, I'm not. Don't you remember all those mean things I said to you?"

"No," she answered.

"Sure you do," I said, taking a moment to remind her of a few. She said softly, "Yes, but those things don't mean anything."

Essie had taken my hurtful words and nailed them to the cross with Jesus, yet I was trying to get her to carry them a bit longer. She wouldn't have it, though. Essie had given those hurtful words to the Lord, offering me forgiveness instead—a wonderful lesson for each of us.

Without getting too deep into the particulars of our divorce, let me just sum it up by saying had I been paying attention early on and throughout, I would have heard what Essie had been telling me. She wanted a simpler life, a marriage similar to what most people have in America.

Essie, who loved being an elementary school teacher, would have been happiest being married to a husband who worked only 40 hours per week, coming home every evening to her and the children. That idea sounds so sweet to me now, but God had other plans. I don't believe Essie ever thought when she married me that I'd pastor a church, be a politician (though this happened after the divorce), and be increasingly active in the community—all in addition to being a full-time engineer. I can't blame her for not wanting that kind of husband. It took a lot of time away from her and the kids. I really wish I could have managed that time better for my family's sake, but I have always believed in service, and when I'm called or asked to do something for somebody, it's difficult to decline. It seems that many opportunities to serve come from God, and I do not ever want to go against His will. Still, looking back, I certainly could have made things more bearable for Essie.

Part of it had to do with my ambition. Once I saw what my parents could accomplish with very little education and means—a happy marriage, a 60-acre farm of their own, a good living, and independence—I determined to be the very best, accomplishing everything I could with my college degree and training. I had a lot of drive inside, causing me to neglect Essie's needs. Perhaps the molestation that happened to me as a boy had something to do with my neglect of Essie as well, but I'll let more qualified minds make that determination.

The only real contention in the divorce agreement concerned my parental visitation rights. The judge declared that I would be allowed to see my children every other weekend, one day during the week, and on holidays per an agreed-upon schedule. I objected to that, of course. Nobody was going to restrict my access to *my* kids. I loved them too much. When the judge called upon me to speak, I said, "Your Honor, I do not ever want to be disrespectful . . . or to get on your bad side . . . but I'm their father, and I'm going to see my children whenever they call me."

The judge said, "Mr. Hearns, you are aware that I could hold you in contempt and that should you violate the agreement made here, you could spend time in jail?"

I said, "Yes, sir. I understand. But if you put me in jail, I won't be able to work and support my children. *You* will have to support them."

That was all he needed to hear. He granted me "reasonable visitation," which seemed to satisfy everybody.

It took some time after the divorce for Essie and me to resume any type of friendship. I suppose that's the natural order of things following such a breakup—allowing the tempest to settle before embarking on new beginnings. Still, my love for Essie never waned; it just took on a different appearance. In some ways, like the bright green grass that appears on the hilltops after a heavy rain, my love for her grew. That's one of the wonderful things about my entire family. We are very close and despite any differences we may have, we include each other in every part of our lives—and Essie, the mother of our children, remained a vital part of our family. When she became ill, we all chipped in to take care of her, even me.

Essie passed from this life to the next on February 6, 2009. I visit her grave often and miss her dearly, but I can now rejoice, knowing she's resting easy in the glorious presence of the Lord, no more cancer and dialysis, only joy.

In recollecting my relationship with Essie, I'm reminded that we must do what we can to repair relationships—to the extent that it depends upon us. We cannot make others forgive us. We can only make ourselves forgive them. The rest we leave with God. And as with all disappointments, we must once again move forward in grace, remembering the good times He has allowed us to share.

CHAPTER TWENTY

# FATHERHOOD

It's hard for me to imagine sometimes that I'm a father six times over. I see my beloved children often, each of them grown, each rich in beauty and talent. Yet, I still have difficulty believing that they are my children. I can say with all honesty that I have never felt so loved as when I've been in their presence. Nothing I've accomplished or done in my adult life could have happened without their grace and support. I honor them here, revealing how each has impacted my life for good in their own special way.

## HENRY JR.

Henry Jr., was born May 16, 1956, while I was at TSU. Essie was still in Mississippi at the time, so I wasn't there for his birth. Honestly, when I heard the news that Essie had finally delivered, I suddenly felt insecure. Questions swirled through my mind. Would I be able to provide for him, or would I need to drop out of college and find a job? Was Essie okay? Did she resent me for not being there? So many things made me feel uneasy. But when I saw his bright face for the first time a couple months later, over summer break, tears of joy filled my eyes, and all that nonsense left me.

I was so happy! Essie was, as well. I was so overcome as I held Henry Jr. for the first time, my young wife beaming as she looked on, that I turned my gaze toward heaven, giving praise to God Almighty for his blessing. After giving thanks to the Lord, I turned to Essie and told her we needed to be together now. She had been attending another college and wanted to finish her degree at that institution, but little Henry's birth changed all of that. After a brief discussion, Essie agreed to transfer in the fall to TSU, where we could be together.

Once back at Tennessee State, we settled in, and Henry Jr. grew to be a strong boy. I remember being in the Army Reserve, and every month, I had to go to a training session. When he was old, enough, about 2 years old, I'd guess, I began taking him with me whenever possible. He loved it! I even bought him his own little uniform with master sergeant stripes. We had a great time with that, lower-ranking soldiers reporting to him at attention and asking for permission to do things just like he was a real master sergeant. That is one of my fondest memories of my oldest child and son.

He lives in Lancaster, not far from my home. I see him often, maybe a couple times each week. We sit and talk about the Bible. He's a preacher just like me, only in a part-time capacity and on the other side of town. Together, we've got the whole city covered for Christ! His full-time job is as a home healthcare provider. He, like all of my children, has a great heart for others, and I'm just so proud of him.

It isn't always easy between us. He's a very determined young man and we are so alike in our thought processes that it sometimes gets in the way of our relationship. But our love for one another isn't affected.

Henry Jr. was a professional boxer at one time. I told all of my children that they needed to do something extracurricular while in school. Henry chose boxing. He became so good at it that he turned professional. He even went to the Golden Gloves competition and at one time was ranked as high as number seven in the world by the World Boxing Association. This all happened about the time his cousin, Tommy "Hitman" Hearns was fighting. They never fought each other, though, as I believe they were in different weight classes.

As a fighter, Henry was very confident but also compassionate. He would sometimes have to fight lesser opponents just coming up, guys who couldn't fight as well he. Although he could have knocked the guys out easily, he didn't like making them look too bad, so he would just win the fight with those opponents, giving them a "fighting chance," as he called it, so they weren't embarrassed. I really appreciated that about him. Still do. He has heart and a lot of respect for people, even his opponents.

Like me, Henry Jr. is a father. He has a beautiful daughter named Shanita, who has blessed me with a great-grandson, Price Wyatt.

## A MESSAGE FROM MY OLDEST SON, HENRY HEARNS JR.

### 2 MY SOMETIMEY DAD
### BY HENRY HEARNS JR.

How do I start a letter about a man that everyone loves, and I call him a "Sometimey Dad?" I will say you have to read all of this. Let me take you back to when I was a boy. Most people would not want a sometimey dad. But to know him, you have to love him. He said a lot of times that he was not the best dad, but he did his best to be with all six of us. He raised six, but I found out he had a lot of other children on the outside of us . . . that I love. Four guys I grew up with, I met when he became a Pastor at the little church.

Let me go back to when we were kids and tell you about a sometimey dad. Sometimes, we would be running late for church. There were five of us at that time: two sisters and two brothers. He would comb our hair. He sat us boys between his legs and pulled the comb through our nappy hair as the other two looked with tears in their eyes and wondered which one was next. Sometimes on Saturdays, he had me cut the grass and sometimes clean the garage. He had the other two help him with the car. After the work, sometimes he would walk us to the store so we could get what we wanted. Sometimes, he would race us back to the house. Sometimes, he would let us win. Sometimes, he picked up Sylvester and outran Hugo and me to the house. When we were bad, sometimes, he would whoop us. Sometimes, he would just talk to us. Sometimes, he took us to the park and sometimes to the movies. Sometimes, his job would have him gone for days. He would say, "Buddy" (that's the nickname he gave me), "Take care of the family." That made me feel like a man. And sometimes, Dad would say to meet his outside children . . . I didn't tell you that their mothers and fathers became my parents, also. Just last week, a lady friend told me she had a car accident, and he pulled her out. She was knocked out, and the car was upside down. "He saved me . . . he is my hero," she said! I must say he is mine, also!

Sometimes, by combing my hair, he taught me to be a dad and help your wife with the children. Sometimes, outside work taught me how to work. Sometimes, after working and going to the store, he taught me we will be paid for the work we do, and to have fun with your family when you can.

Yeah, to my "Sometimey" dad, I want to thank God for you. In football, you made me stay on the team when they wouldn't play me, saying, "Your time will come." It came when the first and second string were taken out. I was put in, and all you could hear was my name being called! I got a reward at the end. The words you told me in high school when I played football have helped me through life. "Don't give up, your time will come. If you quit, you won't see what Jesus has for you."

I love you, and I know your book will be a blessing!! Go with Christ for a better life!!

## VALERIA

Our second child, Valeria, was born June 23, 1958, also while we were still at TSU. Like her big brother, she was a happy child, and her joyful, contagious spirit brightening our home that much more. From the day Valeria could get around on her own, she has asserted her independence. It's one of the things I've admired about her, but also something Essie and I had to watch closely, especially during her teen years, where that independence got her into a few difficulties. Still, she has blossomed into a wonderful woman and I'm so thankful to have her in my life—just a very generous soul.

I can recall a time right after Valeria graduated high school. I had just bought her a dependable new car, about which she was very excited. Around that same time, Gov. Jerry Brown appointed me to a seat on the State's Water Quality Control Board. My appointment meant that I'd have to take a trip to Lake Tahoe for an orientation meeting, but my own car was giving me difficulty. I could have flown, but my wonderful daughter insisted I take her new car. She knew how much I enjoyed road trips and wanted to make sure I didn't miss out on the scenic drive up north. I was so touched by the gesture that I insisted she come with me, which she did—and we had the best time together! We shared good meals together, took in the sights, and even played in the lingering snowpack. That is a very special memory of mine.

Valeria got married in 1978, and I had the honor of giving her away. I also had the privilege of performing the wedding. She gave Essie and I our first two grandchildren, Avril and Andrea. Valeria now lives in Coalinga, California, and works for the Department of Water Resources, oddly enough, and is one of the most financially responsible and moral people I know. She has her father's capacity to think things through, as well. How could I not admire that? And she is a very pretty woman—much like her mother.

## A SPECIAL WORD FROM VALERIA, MY OLDEST DAUGHTER

The world knows my father as Henry, as Mayor, or as Reverend, but to me, he will always be "Daddy." From my earliest recollection, I've known him to be a very compassionate man. I remember back in the days of the Vietnam War when many people did not want anything to do with our brave soldiers and Marines returning home. A lot of those young men could be seen walking along the highways carrying their heavy duffle bags. Whenever Dad saw one of them walking, he would offer them a ride, pray with them, and then give them a little money for their journey.

Daddy loves unconditionally. We children have made our mistakes and have acted inappropriately, but he has always loved us through those times. He would punish us, of course, but he always reminded us that he loved us. He is, and has always been, a wonderful provider. There were six of us children, and not one of us was ever in need of anything. Daddy is also our biggest cheerleader. He is very encouraging! Daddy does whatever he can to build us up! When we were little, although my father was a college-educated engineer, he took side jobs as a janitor to supplement the family income. But that meant he would be away more. He didn't like that. He would take us sometimes so that he could spend time with us. He would hand us rags to clean with, and we'd pretend we were helping him. He worked so hard. And he always made us feel like we were doing a great job, too. Daddy made us feel like we could do anything! He still does. Most importantly, he introduced us to Jesus. He taught us that without Christ, his efforts did not matter. I love you, Dad. You're a wonderful blessing from God! I could not have a better earthly father; it just isn't possible.

—Valeria Hearns-Graves

## THEODORE

I will talk more about my third child, Theodore, in the next chapter, which is dedicated to his memory. But for now, let me just say that he was an extremely creative and intelligent man—born January 15, 1960—who meant the world to me and will forever live in my heart.

## SYLVIA AND SYLVESTER—THE TWINS

The twins—Sylvia and Sylvester—were born November 23, 1961, just 12 minutes apart. They were close in the womb, stayed close at delivery, and have remained close throughout life.

When they were only about 40 or 50 pounds each, I would put one on each of my shoulders and walk around Disneyland. We had so much fun doing that, but they never wanted to get off! Of course, they would climb down for the rides and shows, but if my feet were moving, Sylvia and Sylvester were on my shoulders. They insisted! Sometimes, I would have to lay down the law, telling them that Daddy needed a rest, to which they would oblige begrudgingly. They just loved seeing over the crowds and felt special, somehow riding on my shoulders. I never will forget that fond memory.

Sylvia was a better student then her twin brother, but Sylvester really shined in his high school marching band, where he was a phenomenal base drummer. He fell in love with drums the first time he saw them being played and has never looked back. He is a drummer by profession, even today, playing in a rhythm and blues band. Sylvester is also a very talented artist.

Sylvia followed in her mother's footsteps and became a teacher. She also works with the Black Infant Health Program, where she helps new and future mothers become responsible parents. She's very good at what she does. Sylvia is also creative, as are all of my children, working on the side as a freelance graphic designer. I could not be any prouder as a father of both Sylvia and Sylvester.

## A WORD FROM MY DAUGHTER, SYLVIA

Psalm 37:23 (KJV) says, *"The steps of a good man are ordered by the Lord: and he delighteth in his way."* This has truly been the case for my father, Bishop Henry W. Hearns, Sr. All my life, I've seen a real man of God handle life. As he walked through the lowest valleys and soared to the highest mountaintops, I truly witnessed God's hand in every step to victory! My father is a man of God who isn't afraid to be transparent, allowing God to shine through him.

Dad, I am so proud to say that I'm your daughter (one of the rabbits). Thank you for always keeping it real and for helping me become a woman of God! I can honestly say that I do not know what would have become of me had you not always been there. Thank you for being the last-minute prom date for someone who felt ugly and fat. You turned the sad Cinderella into the Bell of the ball and restored my self-esteem.

I Love You,

—Sylvia Ann Hearns-Simpson (Skibby)

Fatherhood

## A WORD FROM MY YOUNGEST SON, SYLVESTER

### MEMORIES

I remember one Christmas, Dad got me my first "Real" drum kit. It was 1973, which was the year I started playing at church. It was a 3-piece kit (kick, rack, snare with a cymbal mounted on the kick drum). Another Christmas (1977), we went down to L.A., and we got a full kit set up. Later on, down the "timeline," a friend of mine wrote an article on preachers' kids. My dad and I were at the church, and they came and took pictures; this was around 1998. There are so many memories!

When I think back, I think about the travels, trials, and whatnot. I think about Disneyland, movies (Planet of the Apes, Nutty Professor), and driving across the country. I even remember in Pacoima, Dad and I walking across the open field to pick up some items at the little liquor store for junk food as well as walking to Herb's Store, which was just around the corner. Oh, did I mention that we like to eat? Dad, my brothers, and I could "hide some groceries!" We still can!

When I had conflicts with some of my teachers in school, I told him about it, and the rest was "history." I wish I had been a fly on the wall when Dad talked to some of my teachers. I don't know what he told them, but whatever it was, it solved what was wrong with me and with my teachers. Even after he and my mother divorced, he continued to be a part of my life and continues to be . . . even now as an adult.

I know my father as a provider, protector, and personal dentist (LOL). He's been that and more! If I live to see 80 years, I hope I can look and get around as good as he does.

I will close by saying cherish what (who) you have while you still have them.

—Sylvester "Hoss" Hearns

"Hoss" is my nickname my dad gave me.

## ANGELA

Angela, the youngest of my six beautiful children, was born July 13, 1969, not long after Essie and I moved to the Antelope Valley. From the very beginning, Angela was a "daddy's girl." I can recall many times when Angela, who was just an infant or toddler, would be crying over something and both Essie and I would reach for her at the same time. Angela, for whatever reason, always reached for me. Essie would give me a look like, "Why? Why always you?" I loved it, of course, getting one up on Essie. But that was just for fun between us as parents.

Angela has developed into a wonderful woman of God! Her moral character and integrity are second to none. She's a strong woman who lives 100 percent for the Lord.

After graduating high school, Angela went on to earn her bachelor's degree in radio and television production from California State University, Northridge (CSUN). From there, she went on to get her Masters of Social Work (MSW) Degree from the University of California at Los Angeles (UCLA). Angela now works for the Probation Department, helping families of future and past convicts stay together, and she is the minister of music of my church. We have traveled the country together too, me preaching, Angela leading worship. She is also a wonderful singer outside of church, having just released her first album (CD).

As I've aged, Angela has stepped in to assume many of my personal responsibilities. She has become like a personal assistant to me, and for that, I am so grateful, and I know my other children admire that about Angela as well. In fact, all have come alongside of me in my old age to help in some way or another, and I'm so glad I have them all to lean on for support.

Mostly, though, I'm just proud of each of my children for the people they've become. There is nothing greater than the love of a parent, except perhaps the love of a child. My children have taught me that—as has

Jesus, who endured the cross out of love not only for us but for His Father in heaven as well.

## A SPECIAL THOUGHT FROM MY YOUNGEST, ANGELA

There is so much I could say about my father. With each passing day, I find myself learning more from him, always in new and inspiring ways. This man, whom I am blessed to call "Dad," means so many things to me. His presence continues to impact my life in monumental ways, like helping me chart the best path for my life. It was under my father's ministry and preaching that I accepted Christ as my personal Savior when I was only four years old. The anointing the Lord has given him was what made God's plan for salvation clear and desirable enough for such a small child, as I was then, to eagerly invite The Lord Jesus into my life. Even more beautiful is that my father's influence did not stop at my salvation. Because of the example he has set for me with his own life, I am on the same journey with Jesus. Not only is Jesus my Savior, like my father, Jesus is my friend!

My father is also my barometer in regard to marriage. I have used Dad as the standard for the man I choose to marry. He must be of godly character and my best friend, just like my dad. Through my father, I have experienced generosity, gratefulness in difficult times, and unconditional love and acceptance. One time I had a bad acne flair up on my face. When I went to get my goodnight kiss from my father, I offered him the cheek without the acne. He gently turned my face and kissed the acne-side, telling me, "You're still a pretty fox!" Another time, I had to be hospitalized for a couple days. I didn't want to be alone. My father pulled some strings and had another bed put in my hospital room. He stayed with me the entire time! That is my father, a true and faithful friend at all times. I type this with tears, overcome by the love I have for my friend and father. Thank you, Lord, for loving us enough to bless us with such a great Dad.

—Angela Hearns

## FROM ANDREA AND AVRIL, TWO OF MY BELOVED GRANDCHILDREN

I've always known my grandfather to be an extraordinary man. He is like no one else I have known or will ever know. Through words or actions, each encounter with him challenges me to be my best. Grandpa has shown me what it looks like to give God honor and praise when things go well and to hold fast to God when life is difficult. I am so grateful for his outstanding example in my life.

—Andrea

Grandpa, who rose from a sharecropper's son to a civil engineer and the first African-American mayor of Lancaster, sets the standard. Grandpa measures possibility by God, not mankind. I used to feel a lot of pressure to perform something great to meet the standard set by my grandpa; however, I've found, after listening to him (not just looking at his achievements), that, indeed, God is the possibility for greatness. Grandpa still tells me, "Just stay on your road, and the Holy Spirit will lead you in ways that please the Lord!" God's heights are highest and His accomplishments broadest—and as Grandpa adds, His grace is sufficient!

—Avril

CHAPTER TWENTY-ONE

# NO HEART SO STRONG

I remember the night Lisa, my pregnant daughter-in-law, called to say my son Hugo had just hanged himself. The deep and rapid breathing so common with hysteria muffled her words, but I heard enough. Lisa had just found Hugo hanging by his neck from a beam off the back porch of their home, and she thought he was already dead. I'm not sure how, but I remained calm even though the news pierced this loving father's heart. *One of my sons is dead.*

Hugo and Lisa lived just a mile or two from my home on the east side of Lancaster, so I was there within minutes. Still, by the time I got there, the paramedics and fire department had already lowered Theodore to the ground and were desperately trying to revive him. I did what I could to comfort and calm Lisa, who, having found Hugo hanging, convulsed with great distress. Her anguish took such a violent toll on her body that I feared for the child in her womb, that maybe the strain might force her to miscarry. While Lisa cried into my chest, my arms engulfing her, I watched as medics performed CPR on my son. I'm not sure if I could ever adequately explain how it felt as a parent to witness CPR being done on one of my own children, but it was like heaven had suddenly fallen, causing everything to go black for a time. During that dark interlude, all I could see were the memories.

Theodore, or "Hugo" as most people called him, was born January 15, 1960. Essie allowed me to name him, so I chose the name Theodore, which meant *Gift of God*, and Hugo, which meant *bright in mind and spirit*—Theodore Hugo Hearns. To the family, however, he was known as "Boo Boo" for his propensity toward making a mess when he ate.

Hugo possessed a very compassionate spirit, always sensitive to the plight or needs of others. All of my children have that wonderful trait to some degree, but Hugo took it so much further. He *needed* to help others as much as those people needed the help, and he never concerned himself about the costs, particularly to himself. He just had a giant heart for people who were lacking, whether in food, love, money, or whatever. Hugo could not be held back at such times any more than one can hold back the wind when it wants to blow. Helping others just came naturally to him. He was a very affectionate person, especially with regard to his siblings and parents. In fact, he and I were very close friends as well as father and son.

I remember a time when Hugo, who was just turning 40, came to my house and climbed into bed with me. I told him, "Son, you best get your big, rusty self out of my bed! You're a grown man, too big to be doing this!"

Of course, we laughed, but he said, "Daddy, my head hurts. Hold my head so I can sleep."

I said, "Seriously, son—"

But he stopped me and said, "Daddy, I've got a bad headache."

So he crawled up in there and we fell asleep together, me holding my 40-year-old son like he was a scared child. When we woke in the morning, I asked him how he was feeling. He simply smiled and said, "I feel better now. Thanks, Daddy."

That memory is precious to me—still makes me smile.

Although he had great compassion for others, Hugo could also be tough. He was tall like me, had a passion for riding motorcycles, and excelled at athletics, especially football and the martial arts. He had even earned his black belt and mastered the use of nunchucks (two solid wooden sticks, each about a foot long and an inch in diameter, both connected by a short chain, used as a weapon of self-defense). Every year at my birthday, just for fun, we would have arm wrestling and weight-lifting contests to see who was strongest, but by about 16 or 17 years of age, Hugo had me beat.

While still a young man in his mid-to-late 20s, Hugo became partial to alcohol and drug use, at one time even being a functional alcoholic. Fortunately, a man came into my son's life who would lead Hugo back to the Lord. It happened when Theodore's employer sent him to work in Columbus, Ohio. Hugo had attended a Baptist church previously but found it not to his liking and quit going. In Ohio, he started attending Church of God in Christ with a fellow he had met while there. The experience changed his life—a miraculous conversion almost overnight! He called to tell me about it, and I was over the moon with joy. Still, I suppose a part of me was a little curious as to whether he was just telling me what I wanted to hear, remembering, of course, my ploy to get off *the mourner's bench* at the church of my youth. With that in mind, I stopped over in Ohio on a return trip from Washington, DC. Sure enough, Theodore was indeed a changed man! The Holy Spirit had taken hold of him, shaken out his dependence on alcohol and drugs, and restored to him the heart we had all come to love. For that, I praise the Lord!

Despite that conversion, Hugo still struggled with what I believe to be a chemical imbalance in the brain. He was never formally diagnosed with any mental illness and never had a psychological workup, but he and I were close enough that I saw him enter periods of deep depression. Naturally, I was concerned for my son, but his depression seemed only transient and never lasted long. He was a very creative and sensitive person, which may have something to do with the emotions he battled.

Upon his return to California, Hugo met and married Lisa, the mother of his only child, my beautiful granddaughter, Abigail. He even joined a Christian biker club, Soldiers for Jesus. Hugo thoroughly enjoyed riding his old Triumph—which now sits in my garage. His affection for lost souls and his unabashed love of motorcycles endeared him to many members of the club. When they heard Hugo had died, many wept.

Another wonderful thing about my son was his ability to improvise and find new ways of doing things. He worked for several aerospace companies over the course of his short life—Rockwell, Lockheed Martin, and Northrop Grumman—and had become a terrific aircraft mechanic. I can recall a time when he was singled out for his innovative work because of a tool he made that allowed mechanics to apply and tighten hard-to-reach bolts and nuts by themselves, the kind that, until his tool's creation, required two mechanics to install. That development saved his employer quite a bit in high-paid aerospace labor costs. Hugo's ingenuity led his employer to call upon him in situations where other mechanics were having difficulty with a particular task. He really did have a sharp mind.

Well, when my mind finally snapped back to reality, the medics were rushing Hugo away on a gurney, CPR still in progress. It was about that time City Manager Jim Gilley arrived at my side, followed by several others from City Hall. I was mayor at the time, and when the call came into 911 about my son, those who ran the call center felt it imperative to notify key personnel who would be able to mobilize emotional and familial support. And those who responded were so supportive, offering to drive me to the hospital, notify additional family members for me, and so on. But for better or worse, I am wired differently than some. Honestly, though it was my own son who had just been wheeled away by ambulance, who was in all likelihood dead, my thoughts turned immediately to what needed to be done, how I could ease the pain Essie and my other children would surely feel.

For that reason, I chose to drive myself to the hospital. The pragmatist in me, the leader of a city and church, the spiritual head of a family, needed to be alone. I needed to think the whole experience through, not only what had happened, but also what was about to happen. Essie would be devastated. How could a mother feel anything less over the death of her beloved son? His brothers and sisters would be so hurt, mixed feelings about not only his death but also how it happened—suicide by hanging—flowing through their loving hearts. Lisa, his pregnant wife, who was so broken up by the experience, made it to the hospital but later had to leave. What could be done to help her cope?

Somewhere during that 10-minute drive to Antelope Valley Hospital, I began notifying Essie and the children by cellular phone. I'm not sure what exactly I said to each, but each responded as expected—with shock and tears.

It was early evening, sometime around 6 p.m. on January 27, 2002, when doctors pronounced my son, Theodore Hugo Hearns, dead and listed suicide the cause of death. After the painful ordeal at the hospital had ended, after Essie and the kids had come to terms with what had happened, I returned home. That time of solitude gave me cause to reflect on the manner in which Hugo chose to end his own life. How could I, his father and close confidant, have missed the signs? Were there any? He never really talked about his own problems, so I don't know. But there was one thing that should have tipped me off that: something was amiss with him.

Though Hugo did not live with me, he had a key to my house and would often be there when I arrived home from work, sometimes with dinner, sometimes for no apparent reason at all except to check up on me or talk. But one evening, not too long before that fateful day, I pulled into the driveway and clicked the remote for the garage door to open. As the door rose, I saw Hugo inside, pulling on some ropes he had draped over the rafters. He moved aside for me to pull inside, and when I got out of the car, I asked him what he was doing.

He said, "Just checking the strength of the rafters." "Why?" I asked, a curious look on my face.

"No reason. Just bored," I think he answered.

Looking back, perhaps I should have suspected something then, but I would have never guessed one of my children was planning to commit suicide. It never crossed my mind, and I still find it difficult to understand more than a decade later. I also recalled after his death how about three years prior, Hugo said to me that death came fastest by hanging, but only if the rope was positioned correctly around the neck and if the jolt was strong enough. I wish I would have made the connection necessary to intervene in his plan, but it wasn't meant to be. The best thing for everybody is to remember the man he was and forget the regret we might feel. Guilt and regret are too heavy to be carried through life. It happened, it's over, and we must carry on. Good memories, on the other hand, are light and airy, lifting the spirit and brightening the soul.

The Saturday before he killed himself, he was over at my house. I had in my hands a delicious piece of cake, and he wanted a bite. I was joking with him saying, "No. You can't have any."

He said, "Not even a nibble?"

I said, "Now, son, I'm going to let you have a bite, but don't you bite my fingers, boy."

Hugo bit off as much as he could without getting my fingers and we had a good laugh about it. The next evening, he committed suicide. He was just 42 years old. He left a suicide note behind, wherein he lamented about some marital struggles, but knowing my son as I did, I cannot see marital issues alone, causing him to take his life and to leave behind so many who loved him dearly. He was stronger than that most of the time.

Perhaps those struggles just hit him on a bad day when he found himself depressed and obviously despondent. Only God knows for sure.

Hugo's funeral service attracted more than 2,000 people. We had to do a viewing first, allowing the procession of people funneling through to say their last goodbyes before the service, mainly because a large portion of those attending had to sit outside of the church in the overflow area. I suppose many were there to show their support for me as mayor and the mayor's family, but others were there because they had come to know and love my son.

One of the most moving tributes came from Hugo's motorcycle club, Soldiers for Jesus. About 30 or 40 of them rode their bikes to his service, and as they approached, they moved into a special tribute formation similar to "the missing man" used by military aircraft, revving their motors before cutting them off, rolling to a silent stop before the crowd. The gesture touched me greatly, not only because they were honoring my son but also because most of the riders were hardened but redeemed white bikers, my son, of course, being black. And during the viewing, each of them approached Hugo's casket with a hand over their heart. One of the guys— just a huge, mean-looking man—pulled me into him, giving me one of the tightest bear hugs I've ever felt! He told me that they all loved Hugo and that he would be missed, that if I needed anything to call them. Wow! That memory still chokes me up!

Hugo is buried in a plot I had purchased and reserved for myself so my kids wouldn't have to bear the expense of my death. But when Hugo died, I wanted him to have it. I then purchased the adjoining plot for myself, but when Essie died a few years later, we buried her there. It just seemed fitting that her body should rest next to her beloved Hugo.

When I think back over this tragic part of my life, I can only conclude that some things hurt so deeply that they rob us of our breath, of our desire to carry on. But carry on we must, if not for ourselves, then for those who depend upon us. In my case, I had five other children that needed their father's support as they grieved the loss of their dear brother. I did not do it by my strength, however, but by the power of our Father who is in heaven. By His grace, we are saved.

CHAPTER TWENTY-TWO

# AN UNCOMMON KINSHIP

*"A friend loves at all times,
and a brother is born for a time of adversity."*
—Proverbs 17:17 (NIV)

I wanted to take a moment to honor a man who has blessed my life tremendously over the last 20-plus years—Chris Johnson, Senior Pastor of Grace Chapel in Lancaster, California. He is indeed a Proverbs Seventeen friend, a brother in Christ, and a wonderful man of God. Even more, Chris has become like a son to me.

It's difficult to describe the type of relationship the two of us share—that our families share. I would say that our association is a divine appointment orchestrated by God to show the world what Christ-centered love looks like. There are obvious physical differences between us, of course. I'm 82 years old, 6'1", all with a stocky build and black skin; Chris is 42 years old, standing about 5'10" tall, thinly built, and white. But that is only how the world sees us. What I see when I look at Chris Johnson, and what I believe he sees when looking at me, is the love of Christ. Nothing else, and that, in my opinion, is *priceless*.

I first met Chris Johnson in the early 90s, when I was serving my first term as mayor. He had come to an important City Council meeting to show his support for the council in the face of an atheist-led recall effort. Since then, I've come to learn a few things about Chris that have endeared me to him. The first thing I noticed about him was how much he truly cared about the community. Even today, he doesn't just sit back and pray for change to take place. He gets involved, asking God to use him as a vessel for that change. Another wonderful attribute of Chris' is his humility. I don't think I've ever seen him out for glory or selfish gain. When praise is laid upon him, he is quick to lift it and lay it upon another, like a wreath of grace.

There are other characteristics I've come to admire in my dear friend. He thinks everything through carefully, and if it doesn't honor God, he doesn't do it. Chris is a man of great compassion. He has a gift for reaching out to those who have nothing and making them feel like they're worth millions. Chris is also a peacemaker in that he's non-judgmental, putting everybody at ease quickly. He is thoroughly, and I mean that in the truest sense of the word, equipped in the word of God! I call him "a walking talking Bible." And if that weren't enough, he's a great manager, an effective church leader, and a wonderful family man.

One of the things we do together is to meet regularly to pray for each other's families, as well as our city leaders. We know good leaders of cities cause good things to happen within those cities. We are both members of the Antelope Valley Christian Ministers Association (AVCMA), an advisory council for the Sheriff's department in Palmdale (an adjoining city of Lancaster), whose mission is to maintain a productive relationship between the two cities, and the Community Impact Housing Board. We also joined together to help form a community action group that helps young people between the ages of 18 and 25 who have committed their first crime get their sentence delayed for up to one year, giving that person a chance to prove they've only made a mistake. We confide in each other and pray over issues arising within our own churches.

Our two families, though separate entities by birth, have become one in this life, as well. His children have become like nieces and nephews to my older children, and they seem to have adopted me as their grandfather. Only in God's economy could this happen! Only by His loving grace! I recall a time back when my family and I in one car happened to pull alongside Chris and his family in another car as we exited the fairgrounds after a Fourth of July celebration. We had failed to find each other at the crowded event, so when the chance encounter occurred on the way out, we were so happy to see each other that we forgot about the carloads of people behind us. Suddenly, horns started blaring, and one man, if I remember correctly, even gave us a firm rebuke! That is the joy we bring each other.

At least two or three times per year, our families end up together at one or the other's home, enjoying fellowship over food and games. And it's like we are one big family. We have done this so many times now that we help ourselves and know where everything is at the other's house.

Another wonderful aspect to our relationship is that we swap pulpits regularly. Both of us feel it's important to speak at the other's church from time to time to provide a fresh perspective on not only God but life as well. The welcome we each receive from the other's church family is nothing short of inspiring.

The reason I mention all of this is to show what is possible if we look at each other through Christ's eyes, not our own. Again, it's not race that's important; it's *grace*. It's not our differences that matter, but rather our similarities—that we are all made in God's image, hand-crafted out of unspeakable love. Once we discover this and apply it to our lives, our vision begins to change. We begin to see through a prism unclouded by prejudice and selfish ambition. Suddenly, it's no longer my, but thy. It's no longer me but thee. That is the lesson here. That is what this *kinship* with my brother, Chris Johnson, has taught me. I love him for that.

CHAPTER TWENTY-THREE

# THE THINGS I'VE SEEN AND THE LESSONS I'VE LEARNED

**THE THINGS I'VE SEEN**

I've been blessed to have lived at an exciting time in our nation's history. In some ways, I feel as though my life has come full circle. God has brought me from the plantations of segregated Mississippi to a beautiful state of brotherly love. I've witnessed and experienced awesome change in my 82 years!

I've watched as the automobile evolved from a luxury of the rich to a necessity for all, whether as private transportation or public. I've seen biplanes and single-seat propeller-driven aircraft develop into powerful jet-propelled arsenals of war. I've watched as intercontinental travel went from weeks or months by ocean liner to only hours by jetliner. I've watched as 48 states became 50. I've seen the invention of the television, seen vinyl records and the phonograph evolve into digital music, iPods, and MP3s, and I've seen meals that used to take all day to prepare by woodstove now take only minutes by microwave. I've seen human document messengers replaced by fax machines that send images through telephone lines, carbon paper replaced by elaborate copying machines, typewriters and ribbon replaced by laptops, tablets, and printers, and the land-line telephone replaced by mobile devices capable of both voice and data transmission. I've met a King and watched as he and others dreamed big and climbed to the mountaintop, breaking through the barriers of race to transform the lives of so many. I've played a small part in the development of our nation's space program and watched with nervous anticipation as Neil Armstrong and Buzz Aldrin set their feet upon the moon. I've seen a movie star named Reagan challenge The Iron Curtain and Gorbachev, watched as the Berlin Wall came crumbling down, and rejoiced the day apartheid died. As an African-American reared in the racially charged South, I celebrated when men and women of every race, denomination, and state set aside their differences to elect the first African-American president of the United States of America. So much good has happened in my lifetime!

Sadly, I've witnessed tragic events as well. I've seen a hate-filled German tyrant try to exterminate God's chosen people. I've lived to see the most destructive weapon ever created dropped on two Japanese cities, instantly disintegrating hundreds of thousands of people putting the world on notice that we mortals are quite capable of destroying ourselves. I've seen a world at war and the Korean continent divided, splitting families for generations. I wept as Americans opposed to the Vietnam War turned on the American soldiers, Marines, airmen, and sailors who fought there by labeling them "baby killers." I've seen that King I admired so much assassinated on a Memphis balcony. I've seen "free-love" and "live-and-let-live" ideologies erode the Christian principles upon which our nation was founded. I've seen an American president assassinated, his candidate-brother killed years later, and another president impeached. I've seen a Cuban missile crisis and a mysterious illness called AIDS terrify the entire world. I've seen evil commit Rwandan genocide and watched as two Space Shuttles disintegrated in our cobalt skies, killing everybody onboard—one upon liftoff and the other upon reentry. I've lived during the Cold War and watched in horror as the Twin Towers of the World Trade Center crumbled to start the endless War on Terror. Even more heartbreaking, I've watched as the traditional family unit deteriorated from a loving, life-building body into something akin to a brittle and diseased skeleton.

On a more personal level, I've experienced extreme poverty in my youth and middle-class lifestyle in my senior years. I've lived joyfully with and without the comforts of electricity and indoor plumbing. I've loved and lost, succeeded and failed, and I've felt the pain of burying my own child. I've pastored a flock, watched helplessly as some went astray, and delighted when they came back home. I've led, and I've followed, praised my Lord and wanted to curse a few people made in His image, and I've experienced both judgment and grace. I've given and received. I've also experienced the healing power of forgiveness. I've felt the bitter sting of bigotry, served my country honorably during war, and I've fallen short of my own expectations. I've been a child, son, man, husband, father, friend, preacher, politician, and professional. I've felt the crushing effect of heartbreak. Oh, the things I've experienced in my long life!

The great thing about experiencing so much and being witness to so many events and changes is that I've learned a lot about people and some vital lessons about life, some of which I'd like to share in this final chapter.

I was consecrated Bishop on June 24, 2001. Six other bishops, along with Pastor Jack Hayford, participated in the ceremony. First they did a thorough background, questioning other pastors in the community, looking through criminal databases, financial records, church records, and so on. Once the panel was satisfied, they sat me down to grill me on scripture and my life, both past and present. Then the ceremony was held with over 1,000 people in attendance. Several people spoke on my behalf, including City Manager Jim Gilley, council members, pastors, and friends. Then they had me on my knees, anointing me with oil and draping me in the ceremonial robes of bishop. Being consecrated bishop in the Southern Baptist Convention, of which my church is a part, is one of the highest honors a pastor can receive. The Southern Baptist Convention has been a wonderful supporter of our church. Our expansion over the years could not have happened without their spiritual contributions and loans.

We constructed a $3.5 million worship center in May 2005, and they gave us 30 years to pay it off. We'll pay that $1 million balance off before that. Our congregation is better than 2,000 members now. This is done strictly on tithes and offerings. I've been blessed to send out more than 30 ministers working through the church ministry here, and some of them will be ordained, including three women. Every November, I have a meeting at my church to prepare the budget and calendar for the year. I will get with these ministers to see if I can help them in any way. Most of them I can help so they don't end up in a big financial problem and losing their church and church members and all. Our overhead at our church here is large, but the body has no problem sharing it. We don't take up two or three offerings or selling dinners. We are strictly tithes and offerings. The Lord has really blessed the ministry financially, in number, and in spirit. If we would be good stewards, He will take care of the rest. *Seek ye first, the kingdom of heaven and His righteousness, and all the other things will be added to you.* Matthew 6:33(KJV)

I retired from politics in May 2008, which affected me deeply. The outpouring of love shown me by Mayor R. Rex Parris, other city council members, city employees, and the general public meant so much! They even arranged an event in my honor at the John P. Eliopulos Hellenic Center, which was covered by the media. It was just phenomenal! So many of my close friends, former colleagues and family were in attendance, some telling humorous stories about me, others sharing how I had impacted their lives. Had somebody told me when I was just a child sharecropping with my parents and wearing recycled sackcloth for clothing that my life would one day be celebrated, I would have fallen down laughing. But it happened—to the glory of God! Later, they named me Mayor Emeritus, honorary mayor for life and also named the plaza outside City Hall after me. Amazing!

Since retiring, I've gotten even more involved in the local community, accepting seats on the local boards of directors for many companies, to include the American Cancer Society, the United Way, and the Antelope Valley Partners for Health. I continue to serve as an advisor to Lancaster Mayor Parris. I helped start a mentoring program for at-risk students between the ages 8 to 18 with military fathers away at war, those with jailed fathers, and kids who feel unloved or who've been abandoned by their fathers. We called it POP (Pen Or Pencil, the "Pen" standing for penitentiary, and the idea being that the pencil, or education, can keep a child out of the penitentiary). I also co-founded Impact Houses (in partnership with the city), a program that encourages people to better care for their neighborhoods and one that provides community-based gathering places (houses) that serve as clubhouses for neighborhood athletics. I'm also a proud board member of the Antelope Valley Christian Ministers Association and a sponsor and supporter of the Black Infant Health Program, an organization dedicated to lowering the black infant mortality rate, which was a whopping 39 percent in the Antelope Valley at one time but is now down to 14 percent. We've done this through education and by getting African-American women to follow through on health screenings and checkups. I'm also president of the Kingdom Building Fellowship United We Stand, an association of black pastors in the Antelope Valley, a member of the Mayor's Prayer Breakfast board of directors, and lastly, a board member for Grace Resources, a very fruitful homeless outreach.

My point in mentioning these things is to illustrate how retirement from your profession can turn into an opportunity to serve your community. Leisure time is important in your golden years, but retirement doesn't have to mean a sedentary life. Just look through the Bible. Have you ever read of a prophet, disciple, or servant of the Lord retiring? I cannot recall even one because there is always more work to be done. I can honestly say that retirement is proving to be just as rewarding as the rest of my life! Not a day goes by where I'm not blessed in some way or another by the people I meet through service.

Please, please, please, whether black, white, brown, blue, purple, or plaid, do not cast aside your right to vote as if it means nothing. So many people have died giving us that right, people of every ethnicity and creed. We are privileged to be able to affect the outcome of an election with our personal votes. We are blessed that we get to have a say in who leads this great nation. Not every nation allows its citizens a vote.

I registered to vote in Nashville after returning from Korea. That was a very big deal for me, a black man raised in segregated Mississippi. If you remember, blacks in this country were only given the right to vote after the American Civil War. In 1870, Congress ratified the Fifteenth Amendment to the Constitution of the United States, which declared the *"right of citizens of the United States to vote shall not be denied or abridged by the United States or by any state on account of race, color, or previous condition of servitude."* This allowed black men to have a say in their own futures, but it took nearly 100 years for the Fifteenth Amendment to be fully realized.

The South, from where I come, used poll taxes, literacy tests, and many other "preclearance" ways to inhibit voting by blacks.

When it came time for me to register to vote, I registered Republican. At the time, many of the blacks were registering Democrat, even though the Democratic Party seemed to be the primary obstacle to civil rights reform. In the late 50s, I felt the Republican Party—the party of Abraham Lincoln, Harriet Tubman, Booker T. Washington, Teddy Roosevelt, and Dwight Eisenhower—was a better fit for me. I've been a Republican ever since, though I do walk just right of center. Perhaps I am more of a centrist. I'll let my voting record tell that story.

Blacks opinion of the Republican Party changed in the 1960s with the Kennedys, who were prominent Democrats championing equality for all. Protests movements and marches began forcing voting rights changes from the 1957 and 1960 federal voting rights act. The violence against Dr. King and others as they marched peacefully in Selma, Alabama, seemed to turn the tide in America. The fight for equality and the demand for voting rights dominated the news. It was until President Johnson pushed through the Voting Rights Act of 1965 did the southern states finally relent in their tactics, allowing all African Americans above the age of 18—male and female—to register to vote.

In spring 2015, as the country was celebrating the 50th anniversary of the Voting Rights Acts, I was privileged to be invited on a multiple-city bus tour through the South documenting the historic event. "Looking Back to Move Forward" sponsors included the National Alliance of Faith and Justice and the National Parks Department.

I, and others from our POP mentoring group, flew to Washington, DC. Tour members were of different ages and from different areas of the country. Tour Leader Addie Richburg called it a moving classroom.

Just outside of Washington on Route 195, there is a giant confederate flag. We meet the occupants, who told us why they were so excited by the confederate flag. That turned into a really, really involved discussion with us. The white woman who lived there said her grandfather was one of those killed during the Civil War, and she holds it dear to her heart. We made sure she understood that that was her grandfather, not ours.

That brings me to some important lessons I'd like to share with you, things I've learned over the years, some of which came to me the hard way.

## THE LESSONS I'VE LEARNED

If you remember just one thing from this book, remember this: bitterness costs, but love pays dividends. The best defense against bitterness is to understand the cost of bitterness *before* it sinks its rotten roots into you.

In a 2009 *Los Angeles Times article* by Shari Roan entitled, *Bitterness As Mental Illness?* Ms. Roan writes, "Bitter behavior is so common and deeply destructive that some psychiatrists are urging it be identified as a mental illness under the name Post-Traumatic Embitterment Disorder." She quotes a German psychiatrist, Dr. Michael Linden, who said embittered people "feel they have been wronged by someone and are so bitter they can barely function other than to ruminate about their circumstances . . . [They] feel the world has treated them unfairly. It's one step more complex than anger. They're angry plus helpless . . . A profound sense of injustice overtakes them . . . Almost immediately after the traumatic event, they become angry, pessimistic, aggressive, hopeless haters."[16]

Dear brothers and sisters, this type of attitude only serves to hurt everybody—especially the embittered. God addresses this matter directly in Hebrews 12:14-15 (NKJV): *"Pursue peace with all people, and holiness,*

---

[16] Shari Roan, *Bitterness As Mental Illness?*, May 25, 2009, Los Angeles Times, retrieved May 31, 2013, http://www.latimes.com/features/health/la-he-bitterness25-2009may25,0,4544029.story

*without which no one will see the Lord: looking carefully lest anyone fall short of the grace of God; lest any root of bitterness springing up cause trouble, and by this many become defiled."*

Job, a man who faced trials unlike any other, speaks to the "cost and dividends" principle I mentioned earlier in this section. *"One dies in his full strength, being wholly at ease and secure; his pails are full of milk, and the marrow of his bones is moist. Another man dies in the bitterness of his soul, never having eaten with pleasure."* Job 21:23-25 (NKJV)

Like Job, we each encounter injustices that have the potential to imprison us in an attitude of bitterness or to set us free by embracing grace and mercy—the same mercy and grace bestowed upon you and I on the cross at Calvary. Jesus showed us all what LOVE can do, even after being insulted, spat upon, kicked, beaten, bruised, falsely accused and convicted, wrongly discredited, and dragged across the jagged cobblestones of inhumanity! When given the choice, liberate with LOVE—even when it isn't deserved (*especially* when it isn't deserved).

I'm blessed to counsel and mentor a lot of African Americans, and many are bitter about past treatment by whites or from preconceived notions handed down through the generations. I fully understand this. My birth and experiences have given me more opportunities than most to be bitter and resentful, even hateful. But I have refused to take that tack, and it has served me well. My question to those I counsel, when bitterness and hate expose their ugly faces, is usually, "What does it benefit you and your family to carry those feelings in your heart, to feel that way about all people of a certain group?" Most of them get trapped right there. Most have to say, "Nothing."

My approach is to get them to see that there is absolutely no benefit—nothing *positive*—that can be gained from feeling that way, especially if their attitude is one they've adopted because of wrongs suffered by their parents. There is something to be said for the loyalty of a child for their parents, and I can appreciate that, but then there is also a loyalty of the parent for the child that needs to be addressed. The parents have a responsibility to show their children *opportunities*, not obstacles. We become what we think about most. If we think we are doomed, then we are doomed, but by our own thoughts, not by others. The Bible makes that clear, and like all scripture, it's so true. *"For the weapons of our warfare are not carnal but mighty in God for pulling down strongholds, casting down arguments and every high thing that exalts itself against the knowledge of God, bringing every thought into captivity to the obedience of Christ."* 2 Corinthians 10:4-6 (NKJV)

Think you can and you might. Think you can't, however, and you're not likely to even try—and that's just sad. Turn lose all that baggage, and you will be truly free. Dr. King made a statement that relates to what I'm saying. He said, "Hatred paralyzes life; love releases it. *Hatred confuses life; love harmonizes it. Hatred darkens life; love illuminates it."* [17]

Don't let anything like hate drag you down. Don't do it! Otherwise, you'll be dead in the ground one day, buried by your own bitterness toward a lot of people who never did a bad thing to you. Some may have, but most probably not. So I ask again: What good is that? You'll only rob yourself of a lot of love you could have been shown by people you never gave a chance. Let me give you a practical example from my own life.

Back when I first ran for the Lancaster City Council, I took to knocking on doors in every neighborhood, regardless of the demographics. I would, after all, be representing the entire populace of the city, not just my own race, and wanted them to know me personally. But as is often the case in politics, not everyone is on your side. When

---

17 Martin Luther King, Jr., *A Testament of Hope: The Essential Writings and Speeches of Martin Luther King, Jr.*, HarperCollins Publishers 1986, ISBN-13: 9780062509314, Pg. 514

the candidate encounters voter opposition, especially one-on-one and face-to-face, the burden is on the candidate to sway the voter to earn that voter's trust. That said, there was this one lady who, when I knocked on her door, said, "Oh, you're Mr. Hearns. We've already made up our minds who we're voting for on the city council, and it's not going to be you."

My first instinct was to think negatively about her reasoning, that perhaps her decision had been made solely upon race. She was white, after all, and I was black. But my heart, which had experienced so much love from Mrs. McCrary, Mr. Rivers Burks, Capt. Greene, Pastor Chris Johnson, and so many other white people over the years refused to believe it. I held the door for a moment and asked nicely for her to look at my flyer. The flyer talked openly about my campaign and faith. After reading it, the woman asked me in to talk further. Once inside, I saw books that indicated she was a Mormon. Now my first instinct is kicking in again, not because she has somehow wronged me, but because of all the rhetoric I've heard that Mormons do not allow blacks in leadership positions. That may or may not be true, but what I discovered about this woman was that she had made her decision based solely upon a comparison of candidate qualifications, not race. She and her husband felt my opponent was better qualified. Still, as I was leaving her house an hour-and-a-half later, she kindly said, "Mr. Hearns, you do not need to walk my housing tract. Bring 500 flyers. My family and I will walk this tract for you."

That blew my mind! She was no bigot, only a concerned and educated voter. But my heritage of being raised in segregated Mississippi tried to convince me otherwise before I even gave her a chance. This is the problem a lot of African-Americans face today: we are predisposed to think racism when rejected by others of a different race, not necessarily because we have experienced it personally, but because of what has been perpetrated upon our ancestors (and that, in a way, makes *us* racists). This should not be! Had I caved to that predisposition, I would have missed out on her vote, her campaigning for me, and the subsequent friendship that developed between us.

The preponderance of my experience has led me to take each relationship one on one, without prejudice (which means, in essence, not to pre-judge). No group of people has it all right, and no group has it all wrong. Once I internalized and accepted that reality, my love for people grew exponentially. Just look at the wonderful relationships I would have missed out on had I let bitterness reign—if I'd let myself believe that all white people are against me because of what had happened when I was younger and living in Mississippi, or what had happened to my great-grandparents who as you now know were enslaved. Mercy! I would have missed so much!

Don't do that! Get out there and love others, even if they don't love you. I guarantee your life will be much better because of it. *Don't live bitter.* Live better. Ask God to help you with it. He promises to come to your aid, so ask! Being bitter is a form of mental slavery. It keeps you in a cage of your own making, limiting your chances of having meaningful relationships with people who might, if given the chance, enrich your life. If you *do* encounter racism, don't answer with your own racist rebuke. Meet racism with *gracism*. Forgive and Live!

So what I've gleaned from my 82 exciting years on this earth is that we are all subject to adversity, letdowns, mistreatment, failures, injustices, ridicule, racism, and hardships. It doesn't matter whether we're a man or woman, black, white or purple, child, adult or senior citizen, Christian, Muslim or Jew, Republican or Democrat. What matters is our response, internally and externally, to those disappointments. Will we internalize a grudge afterward, becoming bitter or, worse, filled with hate? If so, this grudge will reveal itself outwardly in our attitude, in our relationships with others, and in our walk with God. It will certainly reveal itself in our speech, which has the power to destroy lives, particularly our own! Read this admonition from the apostle James:

> *"The tongue also is a fire, a world of evil among the parts of the body. It corrupts the whole body, sets the whole course of one's life on fire, and is itself set on fire by hell. All kinds of animals, birds, reptiles, and sea creatures are being tamed and have been tamed by mankind, but no human being can tame the tongue. It is a restless evil, full of deadly poison. With the tongue, we praise our Lord and Father, and with it, we curse human beings who have been made in God's likeness. Out of the same mouth come praise and cursing. My brothers and sisters, this should not be."* James 3:6-10 (NIV)

Or, will we accept that in such trials and injustices we are given the chance to demonstrate God's love. He created each of us in His image and died once for all on that cross at Calvary—for sinners and saints alike. That is unconditional love! God showed no favoritism, no inclination or preference for one over another. His love was and is for *all* who are willing to accept it—including those who were stoning Him, spitting upon Him, cursing Him, beating Him, and nailing His flesh to the cross. Some of Christ's last words as he hung painfully from that *tree*—rusted steel stakes piercing His tender skin, a crown of sharp thorns cutting into His brow—were the most soothing ever heard by man: *"Father, forgive them, for they know not what they do."* Luke 23:34 (ESV)

If God, Christ Himself, could forgive under such horrendous and unjust persecution, shouldn't we at least forgive when someone insults us, calls us bad names, cuts us off on the freeway, steals from us, and so on? Doesn't *God* deserve that much from us? He died for all of us, even our offenders. He loved and loves us that much! Shouldn't we reflect that love back upon others? Shouldn't we, too, love our offenders?

> *"But I say to you who hear: Love your enemies, do good to those who hate you, bless those who curse you, and pray for those who spitefully use you. To him who strikes you on the one cheek, offer the other also. And from him who takes away your cloak, do not withhold your tunic either. Give to everyone who asks of you. And from him who takes away your goods, do not ask them back. And just as you want men to do to you, you also do to them likewise.*
>
> *"But if you love those who love you, what credit is that to you? For even sinners love those who love them. And if you do good to those who do good to you, what credit is that to you? For even sinners do the same. And if you lend to those from whom you hope to receive back, what credit is that to you? For even sinners lend to sinners to receive as much back. But love your enemies, do good, and lend, hoping for nothing in return; and your reward will be great, and you will be sons of the Most High. For He is kind to the unthankful and evil. Therefore be merciful, just as your Father also is merciful."*
> Luke 6:27-36 (NKJV)

Those were the words of our Lord to all who would listen, and His entire life on earth was dedicated to living those things out, even unto death. Jesus had every reason to hate, but He chose mercy and love instead. He chose *grace*.

CHAPTER TWENTY-FOUR

# NINETY-ONE AND COUNTING

By God's grace, I'm still here! Much has happened since 2015, and I want to share a few highlights.

Since the first publication of my autobiography in 2015, I have become Pastor-Emeritus of Living Stone Cathedral of Worship. I still serve in any capacity I am asked. My job now, headed towards 92 years of age and counting, is to impart and impact the lives of as many younger pastors, leaders, and anyone else God puts in my path. I have withstood much, as you have read. Since the book's first release almost ten years ago, I have eulogized my last sibling, Douglas, in 2017 and my youngest son, Sylvester, in 2020. All my close friends have gone before me, which included Billy Gray, Charles Robinson, and my engineering buddy, Carlton Lockett. I was so deeply honored to eulogize them all in 2019.

You might think, "Wow, how sad." I have wondered on many occasions what it all means; James Cleveland referred to it as "to see the ships go sailing." But every time the thought comes to mind, PURPOSE quickly takes center stage. The Lord STILL has work for this country preacher to do. No rocking chair for me!

I will continue to represent Him wherever I go. Whether it is speaking behind a pulpit, sharing my story in my dear friend's college class, on the radio, podcasts, or wherever and whenever someone needs a word of encouragement. I am too excited to be able to let folks know that God's grace is sufficient for anything life brings their way. I am living proof! As I take care of His business, He takes care of mine and blesses me beyond words.

I celebrated my 91st birthday this year (2024) with my kids, some of my grandchildren, and all my great-grands. I can't begin to express how grateful I am to The Lord for allowing me to feel His love and the love of my family and so many others. He has blessed me with honors that I never would have imagined, but it reminds me of the Scripture that says, "Eyes have not seen, ears have not heard, neither has it entered into our hearts the things He has prepared for those who love Him." On my 90th birthday, my children sponsored an amazing two-day party in my honor, with hundreds of community leaders and residents in attendance. One visitor, Mr. Kevin Farmer, a top-ranking manager for the United States Department of Agriculture's Soil Conservation Service, announced that Dr. Catherine Armwood at Tennessee State University championed the motion to rename the engineering scholarship after me! Can you believe it? It was also Kevin who researched and found out that I was the first African American civil engineer to be hired by the aforementioned department on January 11, 1960. To God be The Glory!

My friend, I have learned in my years that our trust cannot be placed in political powers, the military, financial status, or those we know who may have significant influence. We can't even place our trust in our religious institutions. All of these things will inevitably disappoint us or will eventually fade away. But God! He was, He is, and He will always be! He promises in His Word that He will never leave you nor forsake you. The Lord Jesus calls YOU His friend. Isn't that something? So, it is my hope that you are inspired and encouraged to NEVER quit and know you are never alone. Your life has a great purpose because God said so. All you have to do is accept His Perfect Gift (John 3:16), and you, too, will experience and be forever changed by God's Amazing Grace.

Hearns Family Photo (2001)

Bishop Hearns' 90th Birthday at Living Stone Cathedral of Worship. Zeta Phi Beta Sorority honors him with gifts. (2023)

Hearns being honored at his 90th Birthday Party Celebration at Lancaster Performing Arts Center, with Mr. Kevin Farmer, from Washington, D.C. (2023)

Interviewed by Pastor Sean Appleton at Hope Chapel (2023)

91st Birthday (2024)

Bishop Hearns ministering at Living Stone Cathedral of Worship (2024)

# ACKNOWLEDGMENTS

First and foremost, I thank God for giving me health, life, and a good mind to get me where I am and for giving me a story to share with others.

Now, I want to acknowledge several people who were instrumental in this project.

**Dr. William Marshall:** Bill continued to encourage me to start and finish this book. He gave me an audio recorder and a fine leather carrier to keep it in; these were efforts to make sure I started, which I eventually did. By God's grace, it is finished. Although Bill is no longer with us, his support and faith in me remain deeply woven into these pages. I honor his legacy with every word written.

**Pastor Chris Johnson:** Chris happens to be a Caucasian brother, yet from my heart, I refer to him as my son in the Gospel. Jokingly, he often says we have "the same ears." Chris, being a very resourceful young man, several years ago conducted a television interview which focused on my life . . . this was the genesis of my autobiography. He connected me with a young writer named David Anthony, who wrote for me.

**David Anthony:** This young man drove back and forth to my house from quite a distance. He asked significant questions, waited for my answers with patience, and embraced my passion for this project. David researched the data I gave him to make sure dates and places matched. We now have a book that I pray blesses all who read it.

**Gwen Cole:** She is much like a daughter to me. Gwen accepted a major task that I would have normally performed so that I could be free to write.

**McKinley Kemp:** McKinley serves as the director for the Black Infant Health Program, an agency I oversee, as I was the recipient of a Los Angeles County grant. McKinley's skill set allowed me to remain worry-free. The agency is still very successful. I've known him since he was about 16 years old; these years have built trust in his ability to get things done.

**Sabrina Scott:** Sabrina is the church administrator who also took the time to receive all my emails of the transcripts and provided copies for me and the publisher. She also gave me her perspective on various areas of parts of the book.

**Dr. Jack Hayford:** I have had the pleasure of knowing Dr. Hayford since the mid-1980s and we become the best of friends. Jack graciously gave of his time to write the foreword to this book, and for this, I am very thankful.

**Pastor Barry Jenkins:** Over a decade ago, Barry served as the chairman of our church's trustee board. He reviewed the drawings for several multi-million dollar projects. The changes he made saved us tens of thousands of dollars. Barry graciously accepted the task of being the first publisher of my book, and I appreciate him to the fullest.

*ACKNOWLEDGMENTS*

**Sharon Egiebor:** At Barry's invitation, Sharon joined the project to help with the fine-tuning of the content. She did a wonderful job. Her attention to detail was greatly appreciated. I am pleased to add her to my collection of friends.

**Willa Robinson:** This dear lady I've had the pleasure of being her pastor for several years, and now I am so thankful to be a client of hers. She works with a spirit of excellence and passion, and I'm grateful she took on the task of publishing this second edition of my book.

**Avril Fuller:** Last but certainly not least, my oldest grandchild, Avril. She helped me to create the title of this book, "How Odds Even." She is a brilliant woman of God, and I am very proud of her.

www.ingramcontent.com/pod-product-compliance
Lightning Source LLC
Chambersburg PA
CBHW051615010526
44107CB00037B/1441/J